Colloquial

Arabic (Levantine)

Colloquial Arabic (Levantine) provides a step-by-step course in Levantine Arabic as it is used today. Combining a user-friendly approach with a thorough treatment of the language, it equips learners with the essential skills needed to communicate confidently and effectively in Levantine Arabic in a broad range of situations. No prior knowledge of the language is required.

Key features include:

- progressive coverage of speaking, listening, reading and writing skills
- structured, jargon-free explanations of grammar
- an extensive range of focused and stimulating exercises
- realistic and entertaining dialogues covering a broad variety of scenarios
- useful vocabulary lists throughout the text
- additional resources available at the back of the book, including a full answer key and bilingual glossaries.

Balanced, comprehensive and rewarding, *Colloquial Arabic (Levantine)* is an indispensable resource both for independent learners and students taking courses in Levantine Arabic.

Colloquials are now supported by FREE AUDIO available online. All audio tracks referenced within the text are free to stream or download from www.routledge.com/cw/colloquials. Recorded by native speakers, the audio complements the book and will help enhance learners' listening and speaking skills.

By the end of this course, you will be at Level B1 of the Common European Framework for Languages and at the Intermediate-Low on the ACTFL proficiency scales.

THE COLLOQUIAL SERIES
Series Adviser: Gary King

The following languages are available in the Colloquial series:

Afrikaans	German	Romanian
Albanian	Greek	Russian
Amharic	Gujarati	Scottish Gaelic
Arabic (Levantine)	Hebrew	Serbian
Arabic of Egypt	Hindi	Slovak
Arabic of the Gulf	Hungarian	Slovene
Basque	Icelandic	Somali
Bengali	Indonesian	Spanish
Breton	Irish	Spanish of Latin America
Bulgarian	Italian	Swahili
Burmese	Japanese	Swedish
Cambodian	Kazakh	Tamil
Cantonese	Korean	Thai
Catalan	Latvian	Tibetan
Chinese (Mandarin)	Lithuanian	Turkish
Croatian	Malay	Ukrainian
Czech	Mongolian	Urdu
Danish	Norwegian	Vietnamese
Dutch	Panjabi	Welsh
English	Persian	Yiddish
Estonian	Polish	Yoruba
Finnish	Portuguese	Zulu (forthcoming)
French	Portuguese of Brazil	

COLLOQUIAL 2s series: *The Next Step in Language Learning*

Chinese	German	Russian
Dutch	Italian	Spanish
French	Portuguese of Brazil	Spanish of Latin America

Colloquials are now supported by FREE AUDIO available online. All audio tracks referenced within the text are free to stream or download from www.routledge.com/cw/colloquials. If you experience any difficulties accessing the audio on the companion website, or still require to purchase a CD, please contact our customer services team through www.routledge.com/info/contact.

Colloquial
Arabic
(Levantine)

The Complete Course
for Beginners

Mohammad Al-Masri

Routledge
Taylor & Francis Group

LONDON AND NEW YORK

First published 2016
by Routledge
2 Park Square, Milton Park, Abingdon, Oxon OX14 4RN

and by Routledge
711 Third Avenue, New York, NY 10017

Routledge is an imprint of the Taylor & Francis Group, an informa business

British Library Cataloguing in Publication Data
A catalogue record for this book is available from the British Library

Library of Congress Cataloging in Publication Data
Al-Masri, Mohammad.
    Colloquial Arabic (Levantine) : the complete course for beginners / Mohammad Al-Masri.
    pages cm. — (The colloquial series)
    Includes bibliographical references and index.
    1. Arabic language–Dialects–Syria. 2. Arabic language–Dialects–Lebanon. 3. Arabic language–Conversation and phrase books–English. 4. Arabic language–Textbooks for foreign speakers–English. I. Title.
    PJ6818.A53 2015
    492.7'82421–dc23

                                                                    2014038212

ISBN: 978-0-415-72685-6 (pbk)
ISBN: 978-1-315-65039-5 (ebk)

Typeset in Avant Garde and Helvetica
by Graphicraft Limited, Hong Kong

Contents

Transliteration key

Table 1 presents Arabic letters. The Arabic writing system is cursive, from right to left. Each letter can have two or four shapes depending on where it connects with other letters. Some letters connect only from one direction – the right direction of course – and thus have two possible shapes. Most Arabic letters connect from right and left and thus have four possible shapes. The shapes are not arbitrary; you will easily be able to figure out the patterns. The following table presents Arabic letters. Column one shows all the letters and their different shapes. Column two gives the name of the letter. Column three shows the transliteration symbol adopted in this book, and column four shows the corresponding sound in English or gives a very brief description of the sound. For a detailed explanation of Arabic sounds, see the Introduction.

Table 2 below presents letters that represent long vowels and diphthongs. Diphthongs are found in words such as 'boy', 'eye', 'out'. Sometimes long vowels can be pronounced short. Usually, short vowels are represented by symbols or diacritics. Arabic has several diacritics that express durational differences of vowels and consonants, and can also express other grammatical functions such as definiteness: whether the noun is definite or indefinite. At this stage, I will present them for help in pronunciation. Detailed explanations will follow in subsequent units. In Table 3, items 1, 2 and 3 express short vowels. Item 4 explicitly indicates the absence of a vowel. Item 5 is written over consonants to indicate that this is a geminate, i.e., the consonant is longer than its single counterpart. This change usually serves a change of meaning. Items 6, 7 and 8 are copies of items 1, 2 and 3 with the addition of an /n/ sound. The last three diacritics serve grammatical functions. The first four essentially serve pronunciation except if they come at the end of nouns in which case, they serve grammatical functions, too. Notice that items 3 and 8 are written under the line. Generally, all diacritics are not used in most written texts (e.g., newspapers, etc.). They are understood by virtue of context.

Table 1 Consonants

Arabic script	*Arabic name*	*Transliteration*	*English closest equivalent*
أ ـأ	hamza	ʔ[1]	t in button (in Cockney pronunciation)
ب بـ ـبـ ـب	baa	b	b as in boy
ت تـ ـتـ ـت	taa	t	t as in table
ث ثـ ـثـ ـث	thaa	th	th as in three
ج جـ ـجـ ـج	jiim	j	j as in jealous
ح حـ ـحـ ـح	Haa	H	breathy voice
خ خـ ـخـ ـخ	xaa	x	ch as in loch
د ـد	daal	d	d as in door
ذ ـذ	dhal	dh	th as in the
ر ـر	rah	r	closest to Spanish r as in pero
ز ـز	zay; zeyn	z	z as in zebra
س سـ ـسـ ـس	siin	s	s as in super
ش شـ ـشـ ـش	shin	sh	sh as in shoes
ص ـص ـصـ صـ	Saad	S	emphatic s
ض ـض ـضـ ضـ	Daad	D	emphatic d
ط ـط	Tah	T	emphatic t
ظ ـظ	DHah	DH	emphatic dh
ع عـ ـعـ ـع	3eyn	3	3eyn
غ غـ ـغـ ـغ	gheyn	gh	the French r
ف فـ ـفـ ـف	faa	f	f as in free
ق قـ ـقـ ـق	qaaf[2]	g	g as in go
ك كـ ـكـ ـك	kaaf	k	k as in kosher
ل لـ ـلـ ـل	laam	l	l as in lamb or as in capable
م مـ ـمـ ـم	miim	m	m as in meet
ن نـ ـنـ ـن	nuun	n	n as in no
ه هـ ـهـ ـه	haa	h	h as in ham
و ـو	waaw	w	w as in window
ي يـ ـيـ ـي	yaa	y	y as in yellow

1 Hamza in most dialects is changed into a vowel /i/, e.g., /raʔyak/ becomes /raayak/: your opinion.

2 This sound is pronounced /q/ in Modern Standard Arabic, /g/ or /ʔ/ in Levantine Arabic.

Table 2 Vowels

		Transliteration			
Arabic script	Arabic name	Short	English equivalent	Long	English equivalent
ا ل	alif	a	a in apart	aa	a in bad
و ﻮ	waaw	u	u in put	uu	oo in boot
و ﻮ	waaw	....	no short form	oo	oa in boat (AmE)
ي ﻴ ﻳ ﻲ	yaa	i	i in it	ii	ea in beat

Table 3 Diacritics in Arabic

	Diacritic	Arabic name	Pronunciation
1	(ﹷ)	fatHah	/a/ as is about
2	(ﹹ)	Dammah	/u/ as in put
3	(ﹻ)	kasrah	/i/ as in kit
4	(ﹿ)	sukuun	no vowel
5	(ﹼ)	shaddah	double the consonant (longer duration)
6	(ﹰ)	tanween fatHah	/an/ as in A̲ntarctica
7	(ﹲ)	tanween Dammah	/un/ the vowel in pu̲t followed by /n/
8	(ﹴ)	tanween kasrah	/in/ in̲timate

Table 4 Diphthongs

Arabic script	Transliteration
و ﻮ	aw
ي ﻴ ﻳ ﻲ	ay; ey

Table 5 Other symbols

Arabic script	Arabic name	Transliteration
ة	taa marbuuTah	t
ى	alif maqSuurah	short vowel /ﹷ/ a variation of ا

ة is pronounced either like /h/ or /t/; ى is pronounced like a short /a/.
Rules will be introduced later.

Exercise 1

To begin, write your first and last names in Arabic. Decide on the letters that make up your name, decide on what connects and from where. Make sure you separate the two names with a space.

Your name _____

Exercise 2

With the help of the charts above, translate each of the following proper names into English.

1 لُبنان	_____	6 ليبيا	_____
2 سوريا	_____	7 ايطاليا	_____
3 الأردن	_____	8 فرنسا	_____
4 فلسطين	_____	9 الكويت	_____
5 اسرائيل	_____		

Exercise 3

Go through the following text in Arabic. Fill in the blanks with the number of times each letter is repeated in all words.

يعتقد كثير من العلماء أنَّ بلاد الشام و الجزيرة العربية و بلاد الرافدين و حوض النيل كانت من المناطق التي استوطن فيها البشر منذ قديم الزمان. فقد نشأت الحضارات الآشورية و السومرية الكنعانية و الفينيقية في بلاد الشام. كما ظهرت أيضاً حضارات العرب الأنباط في مدينتي تدمر في سوريا و البتراء في الأردن. و كانت بلاد الرافدين موطن حضارة نبوخذ نصّر الذي أقام فيها دولة عظيمة. أما مصر فكانت حاضنة الحضارة الفرعونية التي امتدت لسنوات طويلة. و شهدت الجزيرة العربية مولد الجنس العربي المعروف حالياً. فنشأت في اليمن جنوباً مملكة سبأ و حمير. ثم ازدهرت الحضارة العربية قبل الإسلام في مكة. و بعد ظهور الإسلام امتدت الحضارة العربية الإسلامية خارج الجزيرة العربية فوصلت إلى بلاد الشام و العراق و مصر، ثم انتقلت إلى شمال افريقيا و وسطها و حتى الاندلس التي بنى فيها المسلمون حضارة مشرقة عاشت أكثر من أربعمئة عام. و ما زال أكثر العرب يتغنون بهذا الماضي التليد.	ا	ب	ت	ث	ج
	ح	خ	د	ذ	ر
	ز	س	ش	ص	ض
	ط	ظ	ع	غ	ف
	ق	ك	ل	م	ن
	ه	و	ي		

Introduction

This chapter introduces the following topics:

- Arabic sound system
- Pronunciation of Arabic
- Arabic stress
- A note on socio-phonetics
- Consonant clusters

Arabic sound system (Audio 1.1–1.2)

Arabic is a Semitic language. The Semitic language family has only three other living languages in it: Amharic, Hebrew and Maltese. It is therefore likely that your own native language belongs to a different family, and that you will probably be unfamiliar with the Arabic sound system. Arabic has 28 letters that represent consonants and long vowels, and also several other diacritics and symbols to represent short vowels and pronunciation markers. The great majority of these letters, diacritics and symbols are present in all dialects of Arabic. Nonetheless, each dialect tends to have an inventory of its own in which certain sounds are present or absent compared to the common Modern Standard Arabic (MSA). This book is dedicated to Levantine Arabic (LA), a dialect spoken in present-day Syria, Lebanon, Palestine, Jordan and Israel. While LA is the general term to refer to this dialect region, there are also other sub-classifications based on political boundaries, (Shami or Syrian, Lebanese, Palestinian and Jordanian), or based on socio-cultural classifications (urban, rural and Bedouin).

It is beyond the scope of this book to address these classifications in depth, unless necessary for cultural awareness. The dialect adopted in this book is LA – the one that is likely to be understood by *all* people living in the Levant and by a great majority of Arabs. LA is second only to Egyptian Arabic in terms of its spread and intelligibility in the Arab world.

Pronunciation of Arabic

As a point of departure, let us try to understand how words are made up. Linguists use the word "phoneme" to refer to the distinctive sounds that make up words. For example, the word "beat" has four letters: (b, e, a, t) but three distinct sounds – three phonemes: /b, i, t/. It is important to understand the difference between phonemes and letters since phonemes belong to the sound system whereas letters belong to the writing system. When describing sounds, certain parameters are used to describe consonants and vowels of any language. A change in one of the parameters can result in a change of the phoneme, hence altering word meaning or rendering the word meaningless. Below is a more detailed discussion of Arabic consonants and vowels.

Arabic consonants

Generally, consonants are described based on three parameters:

- voicing: whether the vocal folds vibrate (voiced) or not (voiceless) during sound production;
- place of articulation: which speech organs come together, or are activated during sound production;
- manner of articulation: airstream mechanism – complete to minimal air blockage.

Performance exercise: to be able to feel vocal fold vibrations, try producing the two English sounds /s, z/ and see what sets their pronunciation apart. Produce a continuum: start with an /s/ and finish in a /z/, e.g. sssssssszzzzzzz. Now focus on the extra movement you will be making. Cover your ears completely using your palms, and produce the continuum. You will notice that once you move from s to z, you feel a clear increase in the level of noise. This noise is due to the vocal fold vibrations. /s/ and /z/ are only different at this level: /s/ is voiceless whereas /z/ is voiced. Practice this difference as it will be utilized with a number of sounds.

For place of articulation, you need to watch your lips, tongue and teeth. You can observe these movements using a mirror while saying some sounds. Of course, some sounds are produced further back in the vocal tract, which can make them hard to see. But you can still feel the different movements of your tongue.

As for manner of articulation, try pronouncing /t/ and /s/. You will notice that for /t/, air is completely blocked, then completely blown out in an explosive burst, whereas air keeps coming out at almost the same pace for /s/.

Two other parameters are not often mentioned: whether the consonant is oral (produced in the mouth), or nasal (produced in the nose); and whether the consonant is lateral (in which case, the central part of the tongue forms a bulge) or central. Arabic has two nasal consonants /m, n/ and one lateral sound /l/. The distinction between light and dark /l/, as in *capable* and *lamb* respectively, is found in Arabic, though it has nothing to with the lateral.

One additional parameter that is characteristic of Arabic is emphasis: whether the consonant is emphatic. Emphatic consonants are best described by comparing them to their plain counterparts. For example, a plain Arabic /s/ is identical to the English /s/. An emphatic /S/, how- ever, requires the lowering of the tongue in the posterior vocal tract. This new secondary place of articulation results in a new phoneme in Arabic. Arabic has four emphatic consonants (represented in upper case in the transliteration system), usually contrasted with their plain counterparts: /s, S/, /t, T/, /d, D/ and /dh, DH/.

Performance exercise: Produce a continuous /s/ sound, for example, sssssss. Make sure your lips are neutral, that is, not rounded (lips are rounded when you produce the vowel in the word *blue*). As you're producing this sound continuously, lower your lower jaw a little. It can help if you introduce a little lip-rounding along with the jaw-lowering movement. It is likely that you will continue not to feel the difference since plain–emphatic differences are highlighted within a vocalic environment. The least you can get from this exercise is producing a different /S/ sound that feels just a little further back compared to your normal English /s/.

Now that your phonetic taste buds are stirred up a little, it is time to present a more detailed and systematic description of Arabic sounds. I will discuss only the sounds that do not have a generally identical counterpart in English and those which seem to have a counterpart but come with a description of their own. The goal is not to get into the nitty-gritty differences of seemingly identical sounds. For example, there is a strong argument that Arabic /t/ is slightly different from the English /t/. Validating this claim or arguing against it is not within the scope of this discussion since the alleged differences do not render the word unintelligible and do not change it to a different phoneme. And who claims that all English /t/ sounds are identical? Anyway, there are different sociolinguistic levels of variation in LA. The most common of these levels will be presented. It is highly recommended that the learner grasps them. By so doing, learners are more likely to understand faster and to sound more natural.

As illustrated earlier in the transliteration key, each letter in Arabic can come in either two or four shapes depending on its position in a given word. It should be noted here that Arabic writing is cursive whether handwritten or typed: letters can join from the right and left or only from the right. I will present the Arabic alphabet in isolation, along with its transliteration symbol. The pronunciation description is also presented in isolation – that is, free from the effects of co-articulation, which will be briefly discussed in this introduction.

1 ا /ʔ/: the closest to this sound is the glottal plosive. Think of the Cockney pronunciation of the sound /t/ in the word *button*. During the pronunciation of this sound, air is completely blocked below the glottis, and then released abruptly. It is commonly accepted that most English words that begin with a vowel essentially start with a glottal plosive.

Performance exercise: repeat the vowel in "egg" several times. You will notice that you produce a series of glottal plosives with every repetition of the vowel.

2 ث /th/: as in three. This sound is identical to its English counterpart. The reason I am mentioning it here is that its pronunciation sometimes varies between different genders or social classes: urban vs. rural. Most men and most rural people tend to pronounce

this consonant as a (/**th**/: /**thalaathih**/ = three). Most women and most urban people tend to switch to a (/**t**/: /**talaatih**/ = three).

3 ج /**j**/: this is identical to the first sound of the English word "jealous." However, the gender/social class difference mentioned above applies here. Most women and most urban people tend to pronounce this exactly like the *last* sound of the French word "rou*ge*".

4 ح /**H**/: this sound is described as voiceless pharyngeal fricative. It has no English counterpart.

Performance exercise: using your thumb, push against your neck in the area above the glottis and down from the throat. Hold tight, and then blow air on a glass or a mirror so that the surface becomes foggy. Repeat this process and listen well to the sound produced. This is the closest sound to an Arabic /**H**/. Also, notice that when you blow air, the part of your neck pushed against your thumb is the pharynx: the place of articulation where air is making friction to produce the sound.

5 خ /**x**/: this is a sound similar to *ch* in German "loch."

6 ر /**r**/: the Arabic /**r**/ sound is not like any in most dialects of English. Arabic /**r**/ is closer to a trill: the tongue is pulled a little forward, then the tip of the tongue touches the alveolar ridge once. This is the area right behind the upper teeth. The closest is the Spanish /r/ in "pero" meaning "but." You can easily feel the pronunciation of an Arabic /**r**/ by rolling a number of /r/s /rrrrrrr/; any one of them in this production makes a very good Arabic /**r**/.

7 ص /**S**/: this sound is an emphatic counterpart to the English /s/. The primary place of articulation of this sound is the alveolar ridge. When producing an /s/ sound, the tongue goes up to that region. To be able to produce an Arabic /**S**/, you want to produce an English /s/, and then pull your lower jaw just a little bit back. What happens is that you will have to lower the back part of the tongue, which pulls it further back. This back movement is secondary, since the primary constriction is still at the alveolar ridge. But, as explained above, it is hard to feel the difference in the absence of a vowel. This mechanism is still very important since it is pervasive in other Arabic consonants.

8 ض /**D**/: this sound is the emphatic counterpart of the English /d/. The same secondary movement explained above should be applied here.

9 ‌ط /**T**/: this sound is the emphatic counterpart to the English /t/.
10 ‌ظ /**DH**/: this sound is the emphatic counterpart to the first sound in "*the*."

A note that applies to all emphatic consonants is that it helps to produce them in pairs, each along with its plain counterpart, for example, /**s**/ vs. /**S**/. When doing so, you should be able to feel that the emphatic consonant is always a little further back compared to its plain counterpart. Keep in mind that the differences are best highlighted with the help of the vocalic environment. Still, this juxtaposition should help you feel a very important aspect of the difference.

11 ‌ع /**3**/: This sound has no English counterpart. The closest sound to this is the Arabic /**H**/ described above. However, this sound is voiced, i.e., it is accompanied with vocal fold vibrations. Think of the sound one might produce if you were being strangled.
12 ‌غ /**gh**/: voiced velar fricative. This sound is produced in the same place of articulation of an English /g/. The difference is that this sound is a fricative. In /**g**/, the air is completely blocked, then released. In /**gh**/, the constriction is never complete; therefore, the air continues to come out. The closest to this sound is /r/ in French "rouge." One non-speech sound in English that is similar to /**gh**/ is the sound you produce while gargling.

Performance exercise: prepare your vocal tract for the production of an English /g/. While maintaining the same vocal tract configuration, open up the constriction, which must be on the velar area, and produce a continuous sound. This will be closest to the Arabic /**gh**/.

Arabic vowels (Audio 1.3)

Vowels are described based on four parameters:

- height: whether the tongue is in high, middle or low position in relation to the upper jaw;
- frontness: whether the tongue is front, central or back;
- lip rounding: whether lips are rounded or not;
- length: whether the vowel is long or short.

Two phonetic terms are helpful when talking about vowels: quality and quantity. Vowel quality refers to tongue height: how high or low the tongue is during the production of a given vowel. Vowel quantity refers to duration: how much time it takes to produce a certain vowel while maintaining the same quality. For example, the vowels in *beat* and in *bat* are different in terms of quality: each involves a different degree of mouth opening – a different tongue position on the high-low parameter, and in quantity: generally /i/ is longer than /æ/.

LA has four long vowels and four short vowels. Each pair has two vowels that are only different in terms of quantity, not quality. To clarify this point, it is believed among phoneticians that if you were to multiply the vowel in *bit*, you will never get the vowel in *beat* since the two vowels are different not only in terms of quantity but also in terms of quality. But for a native speaker of Arabic, /**nam**/ the imperative form of the verb *to sleep*, and /**naam**/, the past form of the same verb are only phonetically different in terms of the quantity of the vowel; i.e., the fact that the vowel in the second word is only longer than its counterpart in the first word. If this difference is understood, learners of Arabic should not face a great deal of difficulty in learning Arabic vowels.

Duration

Duration of consonants and vowels is very significant in Arabic language. What does this really mean? To further clarify, here is a new phonetic concept: phonemic vs. allophonic variation. A phonemic variation is one that involves the change of a given phoneme. I explained above that this change results either in a new word, or renders a given word meaningless. An allophonic variation does not result in a change of meaning, or in distorting a given word; rather, it introduces a dialectal variation. Let's consider the following examples from English:

> Example 1a: ham vs. hat
> Example 1b: *AmE.* basil vs. *BrE.* basil

In 1a, the phonetic variation is changing the last phoneme: /m/ becomes /t/. This change results in a change of meaning. This is an example of phonemic variation. In 1b, the phonetic variation is changing the first vowel: /eɪ/ becomes /æ/. This change does not result in a change of meaning but a listener who is familiar with English dialectology would be able to tell that the former is typical of American English and the latter is typical of British English.

Arabic obviously does this. But it also utilizes durational differences in the same manner. Vowels that are identical in terms of quality can become different phonemes at the level of quantity. When this difference manifests itself in vowels, we call them long and short vowels. The same durational differences can be utilized for most consonants, in which case, we call them single and geminate. Let's consider the following examples:

Example 2a: **katab**   to write
Example 2b: **kaatab**   to exchange letters (to write back and forth)
Example 3a: **daras**   to study
Example 3b: **darras**   to teach

Obviously, the two words in 2 have a vocalic durational difference, and the two words in 3 have a consonantal durational difference. In both examples, this difference changed word meaning.

Arabic stress (Audio 1.4–1.5)

Stress is the relative prominence on a given syllable in a given word. Stress is phonemic in English but allophonic in Arabic; it changes word meaning in English but it does not do so in Arabic. Consider the following examples:

Example 4a: `present: current; of the time being; gift.
Example 4b: pre`sent: to give something to someone; to give a talk.

The importance of being sensitive to stress in Arabic is the fact that it helps the listener distinguish long from short vowels in a given word. Stress in Arabic is weight-sensitive. This means that the syllable that receives primary stress is generally heavier than other syllables in the same word. Syllable weight is measured by the number, type and position of the segments it is made of: long vowels are heavier than short vowels, which are heavier than consonants. Most of the time, geminates are broken across syllable boundaries. If a word of two or more syllables has equal distribution of weight across syllables, the syllable that receives stress is usually the one that is closest to the beginning of the word, i.e., left-most. These weight calculations drop the last consonant of a given word if the last syllable – having that consonant – is unstressed.

Example 5a: **ku`weyt** Kuwait
Example 5b: **`tuunis** Tunisia
Example 5c: **`liibya** Libya
Example 5d: **`yaman** Yemen
Example 5e: **`qaTar** Qatar

A note on socio-phonetics

Just like many, if not all, other languages, gender, social class, economic class, age, education, ethnic group, social relations, etc. play a role in the selection of a certain language variety. Most of these factors can be leveled or highlighted depending on different factors. Gender, however, remains one area that strongly controls speech varieties. Table 0.1 shows common male and female pronunciations.

Table 0.1 Socio-phonetic variations in Levantine Arabic

		MSA	Levantine (female)	Levantine (male)
1	ث	**th** as in **thalaathih** (three)	t as in table	th as in three
2	ج	**j** as in **jaami3** (mosque)	**jaami3** (j = g in rouge)	j as in jealous
3	ذ	**dh** as in **dhahab** (gold)	d as in door	th as in the
4	ض	**DH** as in **DHarab** (to hit)	dh as in **dharab** (to hit)	DH as in **DHalaam** (darkness)
5	ظ	**DH** as in **DHalaam** (darkness)	**dh** as in **dharab** (to hit)	DH as in **DHalaam** (darkness)
6	ق	**q** as in **qaal** (he said)	ʔ (**ʔaal**)	g (**gaal**)

Notice the case in 4. In general, emphasis as a phonetic feature is more characteristic of male speech from a socio-phonetic point of view. Interdentals /th/, /dh/ and /DH/ are also associated with male speech. Females tend to use the plain, non-emphatic counterparts when they have to pronounce a word with emphatic consonants, and tend to use the alveolar allophones for all interdentals.

Consonant clusters

One of the important issues to consider is consonantal adjacency: the fact that certain consonants are permissible neighbors in some languages/dialects but not in others. For example, Japanese language accepts the sequence of /**ts**/ in word-initial positions but English accepts this sequence only in word-final positions. LA has different types of word-initial consonant clusters. Modern Standard Arabic does not allow consonant clusters in word-initial positions at all. For example, the word for book is /**kitaab**/ in MSA but /**ktaab**/ in LA. As you listen to and read samples of LA, make sure you train yourself to recognize these clusters.

Root morphology

Word structure in Arabic is very systematic; it is almost mathematical. All content words – words that have independent meanings – have roots. This root is usually made up of three consonants, which linguists call *radicals*. Most content words have only three radicals in their roots, although some have more. All derivations of a given a root will have these three radicals. These radicals will always maintain their order regardless of any segments added as required by the different derivations. The derivations in turn follow certain templatic structures. Learning the different structures (ten templates) usually helps in making a learned guess at word meaning, if the root meaning is understood. In subsequent units, the concept of the root will be utilized, especially when new verbs are presented. Consider the following example.

> Example 6: root is k, t, b. Root meaning: to write
> Example 6a: **katab**: he wrote
> Example 6b: **katbat**: she wrote
> Example 6c: **katabu**: they (pl., masc.) wrote
> Example 6d: **kaatib**: writer (sing., masc.)
> Example 6e: **maktuub**: written
> Example 6f: **maktabih**: library
> Example 6g: **ktaab**: book
> Example 6h: **kutub**: books

The list goes on and on. Notice that in every derivation, the new word retains the root and maintains the order of the radicals. The meaning also has something related to the root meaning. In the vocabulary lists in subsequent units (Units One to Five), I will put the roots in brackets wherever a new content word is introduced. After that, readers are expected to be able to figure out the roots on their own.

Finally, wherever necessary, I will explain some phrases that are commonly used in LA. As you know, different languages express the same idea differently and one utterance might carry different meanings. Therefore, issues related to grammar, word order, word choice, cultural setting, history, etc. might sometimes make it impossible for translations to capture both the meaning and the usage. In such cases, further explanations will be provided.

Unit One
أهلاً و سهلاً
ahlan wa sahlan
Welcome!

In this unit, you will learn about:

- Introductions and greetings
- Leave-taking
- Cultural awareness
- Grammar
- Pronouns
- The definite article /il/

 Language points

Introductions and greetings

When meeting people for the first time, you would usually introduce yourself. If there is a mutual friend of two or more people who do not know each other, s/he would be responsible for introducing people to each other. It is polite to introduce yourself to people you talk to for the first time. Greetings are part of introductions. They are common in all languages and cultures. Arab culture is in general full of greeting terminology. Historically, Arab culture placed a great importance on greetings. The Muslim tradition stipulates that "if you were greeted, reply with a better greeting." The social strata remain intact in most Arab communities. These strata have to be recognized and respected. Greetings can vary based on different social relations, most prominently including gender and age differences. Other factors that come into play include the time of day or night, level of endearment, formality, and whether one of the interlocutors has been absent for some time. Politeness is best expressed by the type of greeting one decides to use.

Greetings are conducted using one or more greeting expressions and a handshake. This is almost standard if one is introduced to someone else for the first time. To express a higher level of intimacy or if the two people are older friends, one additional gesture might be used: either exchanging a couple of air kisses while leaning towards the cheeks, or a hug on the right and left shoulders. The hugging gesture might be accompanied with a short light pat on the shoulder. In most communities, this is equally applicable within the same gender. Across-gender relations are different and can vary based on social class. Not observing gender differences in greetings might cause embarrassment or miscommunication. Across genders, women might choose to shake hands or might refuse to do so. So, a man being introduced to a woman for the first time should greet her and see if she extends her hand for a handshake. If she does, politeness dictates that the man should not decline the handshake. If she does not, it is polite on the part of the man not to initiate a handshake gesture. If the woman does not want to shake hands, she will either nod with a smile and verbal greeting or put her palm on her chest and extend only a verbal greeting, or use all of these gestures together.

Often women choose to do so due to a religious belief, fostered by cultural practices, that shaking hands with a foreigner (anyone who's not a relative) is *Haraam* (forbidden from a religious point of view).

Table 1.1 below shows introductions and common greetings in LA and their possible responses, each separated by a semicolon, along with their closest translations and explanations where necessary. Possessive pronouns, which will be introduced shortly, are <u>underlined</u> for clarity.

Table 1.1 Introductions and greetings **(Audio 1.6)**

	Greeting	(Literal) Meaning	Reply	Meaning	Notes
1	**asa`laamu 3a`laykum**	peace be upon you	**wa a`laykum assa`laam**	and peace be upon you (too)	A Muslim greeting that has lost its religious dimension; very common
2	**`marHaba**	hello	**`ahlan wa `sahlan; ah`lein; ya `hala**	welcome	The last one is warmer; possibly suggesting previous knowledge
3	**Sa`baaH il`xeyr**	good morning	**Sa`baaH in`noor; Sa`baaH il`ward**	morning of light; morning of roses	
4	**ma`saa il`xeyr**	good evening	**ma`saa in`noor; ma`saa il`ward**	evening of light; evening of roses	
5	**`ismi . . . ; `ana . . .**	my name is . . . ; I am	**`ahlan wa `sahlan; `tsharrafna; `winni3im**	welcome; we're honored; with all blessings	Second reply is used even if the speaker is singular; third reply is less used by females
6	**`HaDirtak?; `HaDirtik?**	and you are?	**`ana + (name)**	I am + (name)	This is a follow-up; a chance for the new person to introduce him/herself

Table 1.1 (cont'd)

	Greeting	(Literal) Meaning	Reply	Meaning	Notes
7	`intah/`inti min weyn?	where are you from?	`ana min . . .	I am from . . .	mention name of country or town
8	`kiif¹/`keyf il`Haal?	how are you?	al`Hamdu lil`laah; ta`maam; `kwayyis	praise be to God; great; good	There are many more possible responses; will be introduced later
9	`kiif-, `keyf- possessive pronoun	how are . . .	al`Hamdu lil`laah; ta`maam	praise be to Allah; good; perfect	e.g., `kiif<u>ak</u>; `kiif<u>ik</u>; `kiif<u>kum</u>; etc.
10	`kiif/`keyf Haal- possessive pronoun	how are . . .	al`Hamdu lil`laah; ta`maam	praise be to Allah; good; perfect	e.g., kiif `Haal<u>ik</u>; kiif `Haal<u>ak</u>; kiif `Haal<u>kum</u>; etc.[2]

1 /**kiif**/ is more associated with urban pronunciation.
2 See Table 1.3.

Dialogue 1 (Audio 1.7; 1.14–1.15)

Two friends: Ahmed and Laila are meeting. Ahmed introduces his new friend, Salma.

M1:   asa`laamu 3a`laykum.
F1:   wa a`laykum assa`laam, `ahlan wa `sahlan.
M1:   `kiif `Haalik, leyla?
F1:   ta`maam, al`Hamdu lil`laah; intah `kiifak?
M1:   al`Hamdu lil`laah, ana `kwayyis.
F2:   `marHaba, `ana salma.
F1:   ahleyn, `tsharrafna, w `ana leyla.
F2:   `ahlan aaniseh leyla.
F1:   `ahlan biiki.

AHMED: *Peace be upon you!*
LAILA: *And peace be upon you, too. You're welcome.*
AHMAD: *How are you, Laila?*
LAILA: *Great, praise be to God. How are you?*
AHMAD: *Praise be to God. I'm good.*
SALMA: *Hello, I'm Salma.*
LAILA: *Hello, we're honored. I'm Laila.*
SALMA: *Welcome, Ms. Laila.*
LAILA: *Welcome to you.*

Vocabulary

ya   hey; a particle used to get someone's attention

aaniseh (a+n+s)   Ms. (honorific term used for single women)

biiki   with you

Exercise 1

Match the following greetings with the suitable response. Feel free to match more responses to one greeting if you think it is appropriate.

Greetings	Responses	Answers
1 asa`laamu 3a`laykum	a `ana min lubnaan	1 _____
2 Sa`baaH il`xeyr	b wa a`laykum assa`laam	2 _____
3 `inti min weyn?	c al`Hamdu lil`laah; ta`maam; `kwayyis	3 _____
4 `keyf il`Haal?	d Sa`baaH in`noor; Sa`baaH il`ward	4 _____
5 `kiifik?	e al`Hamdu lil`laah	5 _____

Exercise 2

Fill in the blanks with the suitable greeting, response, statement, etc. There can be more than one correct answer.

Greeting		Response
1 ma`saa il`xeyr	A	
2 _____	B	ta`maam
3 _____	C	`ahlan wa `sahlan
4 `ismi `salma	D	
5 `HaDirtak?	E	
6 `kiif<u>ik</u>?	F	
7 _____	G	Sa`baaH in`noor
8 _____	H	`ana min am`riika
9 _____	I	al`Hamdu lil`laah
10 `marHaba	J	

 Leave-taking (Audio 1.8; 1.16–1.17)

Just like introductions are used to start a conversation, leave-taking is a polite form of ending the conversation. There are fewer expressions for taking your leave and ending a conversation. But notice that, just as for greetings, people use more than one expression on the same occasion. In subsequent units, we will learn more advanced ways of taking your leave. Table 1.2 introduces a few very common leave-taking expressions.

Table 1.2 Expressions of leave-taking

	Expression	(Literal) meaning	Reply	Meaning	Notes
1	**is`maH li (masc.); isma`Hii li (fem.)**	give me permission	**it`faDDal (masc.); it`faDDali (fem.)**	you're welcome (to leave)	can use reply in 2 below
2	**bilidhin**	with permission	**ma3 isa`laamih**	with peace	can use reply in 1 above
3	**yallah bay**	let (me say) bye	**bay; bin`shuufak; bin`shuufik**	bye; we will see you	the English term is very common
4	**ba3d idhn<u>ak</u> ba3d idhn<u>ik</u>**	with your permission	**bi amaan allaah allaah ma3ak allaah ma3aaki**	[leave] with the protection of God; God be with you!	very polite; no religious connotations

Dialogue 2 (Audio 1.9; Bonus audio 1)

Tamir wants to leave to go to his class after having lunch with his friends in the cafeteria.

TAAMIR: yallah shabaab, bilidhin.
SALAAH: weyn ya taamir?
TAAMIR: 3indi muHaaDHarah. laazim ?aruuH.
SALAAH: bakkiir.
TAAMIR: laa, laazim ?aruuH, yallah bay.
SALAAH: bi amaan allaah!
TAAMIR: ba3d idhnak.
SALAAH: allaah ma3ak!

TAAMIR: *OK, guys, excuse me.*
SALAAH: *Where are you going, Tamer?*
TAAMIR: *I have a class (lecture), I have to go.*
SALAAH: *Still early.*
TAAMIR: *No, I have to go. OK, bye.*
SALAAH: *With the protection of God!*
TAAMIR: *With your permission.*
SALAAH: *God be with you!*

Vocabulary

shabaab (pl.)(sh+b+b)	guys (sing. = shab: young man; guy)
weyn	where
3ind+i	have + I (this is a preposition, not a verb)
ma3+ak	have/with + you (masc. sing.)
muHaaDHarah (H+aa+DH+r)	lecture
laazim (l+z+m)	must (this is a verbal noun: does not imply a doer)
?aruuH (r+w+H)	I go (the root is /r u H/)
bakkiir (b+k+r)	early (it is early)
yallah	(lit.) let's/let me (in this context, it means "OK")

New expressions

abu ishshabaab: lit., father of/characterized by the youth. This is an honorific used mostly in casual settings. It is most commonly initiated by men (not women) addressing people likely to be of equal or lower status and/or age. People use this term to get someone's attention for some service or to ask a question. This honorific is not used with anyone whose name is known by the caller. For example, you can use this term to get the waiter's attention in a restaurant or a café. This is never used for women, or for elderly people.

> **abu ishshabaab, mumik kaasit shay?**
> Buddy, can I get a cup of tea?

Women usually use **Sabaaya** (sing. **Sabiyyih**, lit. woman) as an equivalent for addressing women.

bakkiir: lit., early. This term is used to express that you want someone to stay longer. It's polite to express that you don't want someone to leave yet.

You've invited some guests to your place and as one of them is getting ready to leave, you might say:

> **bakkiir ya sidi. xalliik ma3na.**
> [It's] early sir, stay with us.

ba3d idhnak/idhnik: lit., with your permission. This is used when someone wants to leave. It's a polite way to indicate leave-taking.

Grammar

The goal of the grammar explanations in this book is to foster understanding of the dialogues presented in each unit. Since the units gradually present more advanced levels of communication in Arabic, grammar targets will be presented accordingly. That is, the reader should expect several grammar targets to be expanded in subsequent units. Additionally, I will be presenting LA grammar along with MSA grammar where deemed appropriate. The reason is twofold: several native speakers naturally use some form of MSA grammar when talking to Arabic language learners, and Arabic grammar is usually written for MSA. It is rather unlikely to find a grammar book for LA, unless it targets learners of this dialect. The grammar targets in this unit are essential for understanding the dialogues and using them.

One last thing is that I will mark stress throughout all examples in the book. **Stress** is the relative prominence given to one or more syllables of a given word. We will largely be dealing with one type of stress: primary stress.

Pronouns (Audio 1.10)

Table 1.3 Pronouns

Pronoun	LA	MSA	Other LA variations
I	`ana	`ana	/`ani/ some rural dialects
we	`iHna	`naHnu	/`niHna/ some Syrian dialects
			/`Hinna/ some Bedouin dialects
you (sing. masc.)	`intah	`anta	/`intih/ rural dialect
you (sing. fem.)	‘inti	`anti	
you (pl. masc.)	`intu	`antum	/`intum/ a rare variant
you (pl. fem.)	`intu	`antun	/`intin/ some rural dialects
he	`huuh	`huwa	
she	`hiih	`hiya	
they (masc.)	`hummih	`hum	
they (fem.)	`hummih	`hun	/`hinnih/ some rural dialects

* Arabic does not have a pronoun for *it*; it uses either *he* or *she* instead. The choice depends on gender.

Arabic word structure is substantially different from that of European languages. In Arabic, pronouns can be independent words or can be part of a given word, in which case we call them possessive pronouns. Possessive pronouns are suffixes that attach to the end of nouns, verbs, prepositions and some question words. I will use one word in LA, **ktaab** *(book)* to present all possessive pronouns. Possessive pronouns are <u>underlined</u> for clarity.

Table 1.4 Possessive pronouns **(Audio 1.11)**

Possessive pronoun	Meaning and possible LA variations
`ktaab<u>i</u>	my book
`ktaab<u>na</u>	our book
`ktaab<u>ak</u>	your book (you: sing. masc.)
`ktaab<u>ik</u>	your book (you: sing. fem.)
`ktaab<u>ku</u>	/`ktaab<u>kum</u>/ or /`ktaab<u>kun</u>/
	your book (you: pl. masc.)
`ktaab<u>ku</u>	/`ktaab<u>kum</u>/ your book (you: pl. fem).
	/`ktaab<u>kin</u>/ is very uncommon
`ktaab<u>uh</u>	his book
`ktaab<u>ha</u>	her book
`ktaab<u>hum</u>	their book (their: masc.)
`ktaab<u>hum</u>	/`ktaab<u>hin</u>/ some rural dialects;
	their book (their: fem.)

Exercise 3

/**kaas**/ means 'cup'. Write in Arabic, using transliteration, each of the following words from English.

Arabic	English
1 _____	her cup
2 _____	my cup
3 _____	our cup
4 _____	his cup
5 _____	their cup (pl. masc.)
6 _____	their cup (pl. fem.)
7 _____	your cup (sing. masc.)
8 _____	your cup (sing. fem.)
9 _____	your cup (pl. masc.)
10 _____	your cup (pl. fem.)

Exercise 4

Use the word `**galam** (pen) with all possessive pronouns. Follow the examples in Table 1.4.

Possessive pronoun	Meaning and possible LA variations
`**galam̲i̲**	my pen
1 _____	_____
2 _____	_____
3 _____	_____
4 _____	_____
5 _____	_____
6 _____	_____
7 _____	_____
8 _____	_____
9 _____	_____

The definite article /il-/ (Audio 1.12)

This is equivalent to the English *the*. This article of course precedes indefinite nouns and makes them definite. It is not the only way however in Arabic to change a noun from indefinite to definite. Other means will be introduced later. See Table 1.5.

Table 1.5 The definite article /**il**/

	Word	In LA	LA /**il-**/	In MSA	MSA /**al-**/
1	the book	`ktaab	lik`taab	ki`taab	alki`taab
2	the pen	`galam	il`galam	`qalam	al`qalam
3	the Arabs	`3arab	il`3arab	`3arab	al`3arab
4	the door	`baab	il`baab	`baab	al`baab
5	the soil; the dirt	`traab	lit`raab	tu`raab	attu`raab
6	the sun	`shams	ish`shams	`shams	ash`shams
7	the summer	`Seyf	iS`Seyf	`Sayf	aS`Sayf
8	sleep (n)	`noom	in`noom	`nawm	an`nawm

Let's explain the issues presented in Table 1.5 beginning with MSA. The definite article here is /**al-**/. You will notice that in examples 1–4, it's simply added to beginning of the noun. In examples 5–8, you will notice that /l/ is dropped and the first consonant of the word in its indefinite form is *geminated*, i.e., doubled. This phenomenon is called assimilation: a tendency in languages whereby one sound is blended into another sound because both of them are pronounced similarly at some level. In this case, /l/ assimilates with all *coronal* sounds: sounds produced in the middle part of the vocal tract. Let's remember that /l/ is pronounced in the alveolar ridge – a coronal position. Therefore, if the definite article precedes a noun that begins with a coronal sound, it deletes and, as compensation, the first sound is geminated. You can see that in examples 1–4, the first sound after the definite article is either produced further forward, *anterior*, or further back, *dorsal*, from /l/.

In LA, the same process described for MSA applies. Additionally, LA speakers switch the order of the two segments of the definite article. (/**il-**/ becomes /**li-**/). If you look closely, you will find the rule for doing so: the word begins with a consonant cluster: two or more consonants without a vowel in between. See examples 1 and 5.

Exercise 5

Add the definite article to each of the following words.

Word	In LA	LA /il-/	In MSA	MSA /al-/
1 the boy	walad	_____	walad	_____
2 the girl	binit	_____	bint	_____
3 the bread	xubiz	_____	xubz	_____
4 the house	daar	_____	daar	_____
5 the oil	zeit	_____	zayt	_____
6 the donkey	Hmaar	_____	Himaar	_____
7 the weapon	slaaH	_____	silaaH	_____
8 the youth	shabaab	_____	shabaab	_____

* Extra credit: See if you can syllabify the words and mark primary stress.

Gender and number agreement

Arabic marks all nouns for gender: masculine and feminine, and for number: singular, dual and plural. Adjectives are also marked following the nouns they modify. Both nouns and adjectives must agree in terms of gender and number. Singular nouns that denote a masculine entity are not marked. Plural nouns and feminine nouns are marked for number and gender. There are, however, numerous nouns that are feminine by default, i.e., by virtue of what they denote. This will be explained in subsequent units. Feminine gender is marked by a suffix /-**ih**/. This suffix sometimes surfaces as /-**it**/. The rule will be introduced later. Proper names are self-explanatory: several feminine names naturally end in a /-**ih**/ but several others do not. Still, adjectives modifying a feminine name require a feminine suffix. Finally, the vowel in this feminine marker suffix is /**i**/ in LA but /**a**/ in MSA; therefore, you might hear some speakers use /-**ih**/ or /-**ah**/ as feminine markers. Always keep in mind that the Arabic writing system often ignores writing symbols for short vowels. Table 1.6 gives some examples of feminine nouns.

Table 1.6 Gender and number agreement **(Audio 1.13)**

	Noun	Masc. sing.	Masc. pl.	Fem. sing.	Fem. pl.
1	engineer	mu`handis	mu`handisiin	mu`handisih	muhandi`saat
1A	tall engineer	mu`handis Ta`wiil	mu`handisiin `Twaal	mu`handisih Ta`wiilih	muhandi`saat Tawii`laat
2	teacher	`m3allim	m3al`lmiin	`m3allmih	m3al`lmaat
2A	short teacher	`m3allim ga`Siir	m3al`lmiin gSaar	`m3allmih ga`Siirih	m3al`lmaat gaSii`raat

At this point, it is useful to know that the masculine plural suffix is /-**iin**/ and the feminine plural suffix is /-**aat**/. However, Arabic does use a great deal of irregular plurals – more so for masculine rather than feminine plurals. Notice also that the feminine plural marker /-**aat**/ is sufficient to denote both gender and number, so no need to use the feminine marker /-**ih**/ and the plural suffix /-**aat**/.

Exercise 6

Translate each of the following phrases into Arabic.

English	*Arabic*
1 a big door	_____
2 a big cup	_____
3 a tall teacher (masc.)	_____
4 a tall teacher (fem.)	_____
5 a short engineer (masc.)	_____
6 a short engineer (fem.)	_____
7 a small door	_____
8 a tall girl	_____
9 a big house	_____
10 a big book	_____

Exercise 7

Write a proper reply to each of the following greetings:

1 Sa`baaH il`xeyr
2 `keyf il`Haal?
3 `ana kw`ayyis. `ana `ismi lamiis.
4 `inti min weyn?
5 `ahlan wa `sahlan.
6 wa `inta min weyn?

Exercise 8

Salma and Mariam are friends. Salma wants to introduce Mustafa to Mariam. Write a dialogue that serves this function.

Cultural point

As mentioned above, Levantine dialect is abundant with greetings. There are very general practices that are deemed appropriate on a wide range of occasions and there are also a few very fine subtleties that you need to be aware of. For example, observing gender-related protocol is very important especially if you are visiting a family or if you are in a more traditional rural or Bedouin setting. Some of the best ways to advance your understanding of these cultural practices is to have a friend or a classmate whom you can ask. If this person is familiar with Western culture, that would be an added benefit. Another very good thing is to observe closely how people react once they meet. Most people will welcome your questions and be more than willing to answer. Here are a few other tips:

- In terms of dress, pants and trousers are acceptable types of dress for both men and women. Shorts are not favorable. Short sleeves are more common for men than for women. On college campuses, these differences are not closely observed due to the diversity on campus.
- It is OK for people to ask about things usually considered personal in Western culture. People are likely to ask about your religion, whether you're married or not, your income, your family members, etc. You can give general answers that do not really reveal much. If visiting any country in the Levantine area other than Israel, it's usually prudent not to reveal your religion if you are Jewish or atheist; people are generally more tolerant of the Christian faith.
- If sitting in a group, make sure the soles of your shoes are not facing anyone's face: it's deemed impolite.
- No public displays of affection. These are frowned upon.
- It's OK for people of the same gender to be walking around holding hands. It is just a sign of friendship.
- The elderly are always respected. It is polite to give up one's seat for an elderly person, or for a woman if in a crowded bus, class, waiting area, etc.
- If going into a place of worship, women and girls must cover themselves up. Only their faces and hands should be visible.

Unit Two

هذا العالم

haadha il3aalam

This world

In this unit, you will learn about:

- Honorifics
- Nationalities and hometowns
- Cultural awareness
- Subject pronouns
- Nisba adjectives
- Regular plurals
- High frequency connectors (and, or, but)
- Identifying the letters (ا، و، ي، ب، ت، ث، ج، ح، خ)
- Identifying the short vowels: **fatHah** (ﹷ), **Dammah** (ﹹ), **kasarah** (ﹻ)

Honorifics

Each culture has its way of expressing respect. One of the major ways of showing respect in Levantine culture is the use of honorifics. Honorifics are often used whenever the relationship between the interlocutors is not really equal. This can be due to various differences: social, economic or educational. Also gender and age differences are major reasons for using honorifics. Generally, if you are introduced to someone for the first time, formality and respect require the use of the proper "title." LA speakers rarely address people using their first names when these people are older, or more educated. Almost all married people with children expect to be addressed with some title. You can address students or other single people of relatively similar age to yours by their first names. Another thing to keep in mind that these honorifics are followed by the person's first name, not by their family name. So, if you were talking to Dr. Noam Chomsky, you would formally use Dr. Chomsky in English but *duktoor Noam* in Arabic. It is worth mentioning that LA uses a lot more honorifics compared to English. Therefore, translations will focus on the functional meaning with explanations where necessary. Table 2.1 below shows the most common ones.

Table 2.1 Honorifics **(Audio 1.18)**

	Honorific	(Literal) meaning	Notes
1	`ax; `uxt	brother; sister	no indication of blood relationship
2	`aaniseh	Miss	for an unmarried woman
3	sitt	Mrs.	for a married or divorced woman
4	ma`daam	Madam	for a married woman; has an indication of higher social class
5	us`taadh; us`taadhih	teacher (masc.) teacher (fem.)	usually used in the academic field
6	`xaaluh; `xaaltuh	uncle; aunt	by a younger person to an older one; no indication of blood relationship
7	`3ammuh; `3ammtuh	uncle; aunt	by a younger person to an older one; no indication of blood relationship
8	`Hajji; Haj`jiyyih	pilgrim	usually used with elderly people; the term has lost its religious connotation
9	abu . . . um . . . or im . . .	father of . . .; mother of . . .	these words are followed by the name of the eldest son or (less commonly) eldest daughter; it is used to talk to married people
10	duk`toor; duk`toorah	doctor (masc., fem.); professor (masc., fem.)	for a doctor or PhD holders
11	mu`handis; mu`handisih	engineer (masc., fem.)	for all engineers

Dialogue 1 (Audio 1.19)

Dr. Faisal is a university professor being greeted at a formal dinner. Samia introduces him to the table.

SAAMYA:	ahlan duktoor feySal.
DUKTOOR FEYSAL:	ahlan biiki. ahlan uxt saamya.
SAAMYA:	tfaDDal, duktoor.
DUKTOOR FEYSAL:	shukran!
SAAMYA:	haadha ustaadh 3ammaar, wa haay madaam wafaaʔ.
DUKTOOR FEYSAL:	tsharrafna.
SAAMYA:	wa haadha duktoor xaalid, wa muhandisih aamnih.
DUKTOOR FEYSAL:	ahlan wa sahlan. min weyn duktoor xaalid?
DUKTOOR XAALID:	ana min naablis. ilmadaam min maadaba.
DUKTOOR FEYSAL:	wa ana min naablis kamaan. ustaadh 3ammar intah min weyn?
3AMMAAR:	ana min irbid, wa sitt lamya min ilbatra

SAMIA:	*Welcome Dr. Faisal.*
FAISAL:	*Welcome to you too. You're welcome sister Samia.*
SAMIA:	*Welcome, doctor.* (Functionally, this is inviting him to take a seat)
FAISAL:	*Thank you!*
SAMIA:	*This is Mr. Ammar, and this is Mrs. Wafa.*
FAISAL:	*I'm honored.*
SAMIA:	*And this is Dr. Khalid, and Engineer Amneh.*
FAISAL:	*Welcome! Where are you from Dr. Khalid?*
DR. KHALID:	*I'm from Nablus. Madam (Engineer Amneh) is from Madaba.*
FAISAL:	*I am from Nablus, also. Mr. Ammar, where are you from?*
AMMAR:	*I'm from Irbid, and Mrs. Lamia is from Petra.*

Vocabulary

min   from

kamaan   again; too

shukran thanks

itfaDDal there you go (offering someone something)

New expressions

itfaDDal: lit., be kind; be generous. Used as a statement, this is a polite invitation for someone to come inside a place or to do something. For example, if you're visiting someone, he/she can say *tfaDDal* once you knock on the door or ring the bell. A teacher handing out some worksheets can say *tfaDDal* to each one of her/his students. Once food is offered, the host invites guests to start eating by saying *tfaDDalu*.

You borrowed someone's pen to write something. Having finished, you give it back and say:

  itfaDDal. shukran.
  There you go, thanks.

itfaDDal?: lit., be kind; be generous. With a question intonation, this expression changes meaning. It now means "what can I do for you?" or "how can I help?" For example, if someone is phoning asking to speak to you, you can respond by saying *tfaDDal?* This will prompt the caller to say what he/she wants.

You're walking down the street and someone stops you to ask you something, you say:

  itfaDDal, 3indak su?aal?
  What can I do for you, do you have a question?

Exercise 1

You are a college student (male) going with your friend Khalid to visit his family. Khalid gave you a list of his family members. Read the names and the descriptions for each of them and write how you will greet each one of them properly. You have never met them before.

1 Abu Khalid is the father.
2 Um Khalid is the mother.
3 Laila is Khalid's sister. She is a college student.
4 Salim is Khalid's youngest brother.
5 Um Omar is Khalid's grandmother. She's an old lady.

Exercise 2

If you were a female student going to visit the same family with your female friend, would any of the greetings above change? Explain.

Nationalities and hometowns (nisba forms)

Nationalities and hometowns are some of the ways people connect. It is a very common way of establishing a relationship, bonding with people and finding new topics to talk about. LA uses the suffix /-i/ with the country/town name to refer to someone who belongs to it. For a female, the feminine marker is also needed, and then you end up with /-yih/. In Arabic grammar, this is generally referred to as *nisba* form: generally "belonging." This term captures more than nationalities. There are of course a few exceptions to this nisba rule but it covers a great deal of nationalities. One of the very common exceptions is deleting the marker if the country/town name already ends in an /-i/ or /-yih/ in Arabic. If the country/town name ends in /-yih/, it is deemed feminine; therefore, you will need to delete the feminine marker when referring to a male, so the nisba form becomes shorter than the country/town name. Another important point to notice here is that some country/town names start with the Arabic definite article /-al/ or /-il/. In this case, you will need to delete it. Table 2.2 presents examples of some nationalities.

Table 2.2 Common nationalities **(Audio 1.20)**

	Country/town	Nisba form (masc.)	Nisba form (fem.)	Translation
1	`urdun	`urduni	urdun`niiyih	Jordanian
2	am`riika; a`mirika	am`riiki	am`riikiyih	American
3	al`maghrib	`maghribi	`maghribiyih	Moroccan
4	barî`Taanyia	barî`Taani	barî`Taaniyih	British
5	`s3uudiyyih	s3uudi	s3uudiyyih	Saudi
6	`suuriyya	`suuri	suu`riiyih	Syrian
7	fa`ransa	fa`ransi	fa`ransiyih	French
8	falas`Tiin	falas`Tiini	falas`Tiiniyih	Palestinian
9	lub`naan	lub`naani	lub`naaniyih	Lebanese
10	maSr	`maSri	maS`riyih	Egyptian

Dialogue 2 (Audio 1.21)

In the first class of the semester, the teacher introduces himself and says where he is from. Then each student introduces himself/herself. Notice how names of towns and countries are pronounced differently in Arabic. Also notice the gender marker /-**ah**/ or /-**at**/ suffixed to the end of the masculine noun.

USTAADH 3UMAR:	ahlan shabaab. ana ismii 3umar, wa ana urdini min 3ammaan.
TAALIB 1:	ana ismii maikil, wa ana amriiki min waashinTun.
TAALIBAH 2:	ana ilizabith, wa ana amriikiyah min uklahooma.
TAALIBAH 3:	ana meyri, ana bariTaanyah min landan.
TAALIBAH 4:	ismii treysi, ana min madiinat nyuu yoork.
TAALIB 5:	ana joon, wa ana min kanada, min madiinat moontiryaal.
TAALIBAH 6:	ana janifar, wa ana min baariss fi faransa.
USTAATDH 3UMAR:	alhan biikum fi ilurdun.

TEACHER OMAR:	*Welcome guys. My name is Omar. And I am a Jordanian from Amman.*
STUDENT 1:	*My name is Michael. I am an American from Washington.*

STUDENT 2:	*I am Elizabeth, and I'm an American from Oklahoma.*
STUDENT 3:	*I am Mary, I'm British from London.*
STUDENT 4:	*My name is Tracy, I'm from the city of New York.*
STUDENT 5:	*I am John, and I'm from Canada, from the city of Montreal.*
STUDENT 6:	*I'm Jennifer, and I'm from Paris in France.*
TEACHER OMAR:	*Welcome to Jordan all of you.*

Vocabulary

ism+ii	name + my (my name)
madiinah/madiinat (m+d+n)	city/town
fi	in
bi+k+um	with + you + pl. (with you all)

Exercise 3a

Fill in the following table with nisba forms.

	Country/town	Nisba form (masc.)	Nisba form (fem.)	Translation
1	**al`maanya**			
2	**`ruusya**			
3	**falas`Tiin**			
4	**alja`zaaʔir**			
5	**almak`siik**			
6	**israa`iil**			
7	**qa`Tar**			
8	**is`baannya**			
9	**`kanada**			
10	**3am`maan**			

Exercise 3b

Can you write the feminine and masculine plurals? The irregular ones have been provided.

	Country/town	Nisba form (masc, pl)	Nisba form (fem, pl)	Translation
1	**al`maanya**	al`maan	_____	_____
2	**`ruusya**	ruus	_____	_____
3	**falas`Tiin**	_____	_____	_____
4	**alja`zaa?ir**	_____	_____	_____
5	**almak`siik**	_____	_____	_____
6	**israa`iil**	_____	_____	_____
7	**`qaTar**	_____	_____	_____
8	**is`baannya**	_____	_____	_____
9	**`kanada**	_____	_____	_____
10	**3am`maan**	_____	_____	_____

Grammar

Subject pronouns

Subject pronouns are simply units that replace nouns. In Arabic, these are contrasted with the object and possessive pronouns. A subject pronoun can function independently just like the head noun of a sentence. Subject pronouns do not have to attach to a word. Table 2.3 introduces subject pronouns.

Table 2.3 Subject pronouns

Pronoun	Translation	Notes
`ana; `aani; `ani	I	first is most common; second and third are rural variants
`iHna; `niHna; `Hinna	we	second is common in Syrian; third is Bedouin
`intah; `intih	you (sing. masc.)	first is common; second is rural
`inti	you (sing. fem.)	
`intum	you (pl. masc.)	sometimes used to refer to pl. fem. especially in urban dialects
`intin	you (pl. fem.)	less commonly used
`huwwa; huuh	he; it (masc.)	
`hiyya; hiih	she; it (fem.)	
`humma; hum	they (pl. masc.)	sometimes used to refer to pl. fem. especially in urban dialects
`hinnih	they (pl. fem.)	less commonly used

Exercise 4

Translate the following statements into Arabic. At this point, feel free to use transliteration.

1 I am a teacher.
2 She is a teacher.
3 You are an engineer.
4 You are American.
5 He is Lebanese.

Regular plurals

Arabic exhibits simple rules for the formation of regular plurals. Irregular plurals, however, remain abundant in the language. Since adjectives have to agree with the nouns they modify in terms of number, the plural rule becomes very productive. While nouns show clear deviation from the rule, adjectives normally follow the plural rule more closely. That is, adjectives that take irregular plural markers are less common. Arabic also gives different plural suffixes to masculine and feminine nouns. Here is the rule: add the suffix /-**iin**/ to masculine singular nouns; for feminine plurals, drop the feminine marker (/-**ah**/; /-**at**/) from the end of the feminine singular noun, then add the suffix /-**aat**/. Non-human and inanimate nouns obtain their plurals depending on the perceived gender, so to speak. However, rarely do non-human or inanimate masculine nouns follow the regular plural rule. This is most efficiently learnt by practice. Adjectives modifying plural nouns take the regular plural maker: i.e., if the noun is masculine plural, the adjective is masculine plural, too. Adjectives modifying inanimate or non-human plurals take the feminine plural suffix /-**aat**/. As you go through the following examples (see Table 2.4), recall that Arabic dialects have considerable variations in terms of short vowels. Since Arabic words are based on three consonants (see Introduction), short vowels might change.

Table 2.4 Arabic regular plurals **(Audio 1.22)**

English	Singular	Plural	Notes
teacher (masc.)	`m3allim	m3a`lmiin	**ma3aa`liim** is also possible
teacher (fem.)	`m3allmah; `m3allmih	m3al`maat	
engineer (masc.)	mu`handis	muhandi`siin	
engineer (fem.)	mu`handisah; mu`handisih	muhandi`saat	
car	say`yaarah	sayya`raat	
cab	`taksi	taksy`yaat	**ta`kaasi** is also possible

High frequency connectors (and, or, but)
(Audio 1.23)

The meanings and functions served by these connectors are mostly similar to those served in MSA or in other languages. Some of them can be contracted and some functions can be served by more than one particle, as is the case with most connectors. Table 2.5 below presents these common particles.

Table 2.5 and, or, but

English	LA	Notes
and	**wa; uu; u**	the second variant is a contracted form in a stressed position; the third is contracted in an unstressed position
or	**aw; yaa . . . yaa**	the second is closer to the construction either . . . or
but	**laakin; bass**	the first is MSA but heavily used in LA

You will notice that "and" gets contracted, mostly to /**u**/ in most dialogues. This is how it is pronounced in regular speech.

Exercise 5

Translate each of the following statements into Arabic. Feel free to use transliteration.

1 We are teachers.
2 I have three cars.
3 I am Jordanian but he is American.
4 She is Palestinian and he is British.
5 They are Canadian girls.

Identifying the letters (خ ،ح ،ج ،ث ،ت ،ب ،ي ،و ،ا)

As of this unit forward, we will be practicing letters of the Arabic alphabet. The goal of these exercises is to familiarize the reader with Arabic script, and also to be able to read simple Arabic phrases, road signs, items on a menu and other things related to everyday life. For the letters of the alphabet, refer to the transliteration key. As we go through these letters, I will be presenting some explanations necessary to the understanding of the Arabic alphabet.

Arabic writing is recursive. Start always from the right and go to left. Once writing the letter is completed, lift the pen to add the dots and other short vowels if applicable. Also keep in mind which letters are written completely over the line, and which ones are split over and under the line.

For this group of letters, the first one is a vowel. Therefore, it comes with its own surprises. If the letter stands by itself, with no diacritics, it is usually pronounced as long vowel /**aa**/. Sometimes, this letter can be a hamza (أ), as shown in the transliteration key. In other cases, it can receive a diacritic, which could change its meaning. Here are the variations:

أ **hamzat fatH**: much like a short vowel /**a**/, e.g., the first sound of the pronoun (**ana** = I).
أ **hamzat Damm**: much like a short vowel /**u**/, e.g., the first sound of (umm = mother of).
إ **hamzat kasr**: much like a short vowel /**i**/, e.g., the first sound of (intih = you [masc. sing.]).

To help you remember these different types, you might recall that the names of the three types here are the first three in Table 3 in the transliteration key. If the small diacritic (ء) is written on top of (ا), it is a short /**a**/; if a Dammah is added, it becomes a short /**u**/. If the diacritic (ء) is written under the (ا), it is pronounced as a short /**i**/.

Sometimes, the diacritic is written directly on the line following a word-final (ا). This is an indication that the vowel must be lengthened. Word-final lengthening of (ا) is more common in MSA, rather than LA.

In LA, as in many dialects of Arabic, a hamza is turned into a short vowel in many cases.

Finally, short vowels are pronounced the way they are described, and shaddah (ـّ) is a lengthening of the consonant that receives it.

Exercise 6

Write each of the following letters three times:

ا	ث
و	ج
ي	ح
ب	خ
ت	

Exercise 7 (**Bonus audio 3**)

Join the following letters to make up words. Add the short vowels where appropriate (where they appear on the letters in isolation). Refer to the transliteration key if you need help. Again, make sure you start from right to left. Read the words and practise them aloud.

1 ب ا ب (door)
2 ث ا ب ت (fixed; proper name)
3 ب ت ح ب (she likes; she loves)
4 ح ا ج (pilgrim; honorific title)
5 خ ا ب (he failed)
6 ب ا ت (he slept)
7 ج ي ب (bring [imp.])
8 ث و ب (dress; robe)
9 ج و ب ا (Juba [city in Sudan])
10 ح ب ي ب (beloved [masc.])

Exercise 8

Identify the letters (خ، ح، ج، ث، ت، ب، ي، و، ا) in the following paragraph. There is no need to worry about the letters you do not know at this time.

ا	و	ي	ب	ت	ث	ج	ح	خ

العراق دولة تقع في شمال غرب العالم العربي. يبلغ عدد سكان العراق حوالي ستة و ثلاثين مليون نسمة. يحده من الشمال تركيا، و من الغرب إيران، من الجنوب الكويت و السعودية ومن الشرق سوريا و الأردن. تعتبر دولة العراق واحدة من أقدم الحضارات في العالم. فقد قامت حضارة ما بين بلاد الرافدين قبل أكثر من ثمانية آلاف سنة، و في العراق تم اختراع الكتابة المسمارية و كان السومريون من أول الشعوب التي حكمت هذه البلاد. و كانت العراق أيضاً مهداً للحضارة الاكادية، و الآشورية و البابلية. و بعد ظهور الإسلام انتقلت عاصمة الدولة الإسلامية اليها في زمن الدولة العباسية. من أهم مدنها بغداد، الموصل، كربلاء، و البصرة في الجنوب.

Cultural point

The word **nisba** or **nisbah** comes from the root **n+s+b**, which in Arabic refers to origin. Most people in the Arab world take pride in tracing their origins back to their ancestors. Many families keep track of their family trees. This interest in one's origin can be traced back to the pre-Islamic era. The science of origins (**3ilm ala?nsaab**) is thriving in the Arab world. Some tribes trace their ancestry further back than medieval times. Others claim they are direct descendants of Prophet Mohammad's Companions. There are several cultural reasons for this interest in people's origins, such as showing cultural heritage and depth, being attributed to historical heroes, belonging to a prominent tribe and signaling long residence and ownership of a given land.

Other nisba classifications have to do with place of origin as opposed to tribal origins. In most LA countries, people who come from villages are called **fallaaH** (pl. **fallaHiin**); if they are from the desert, they are called **badawi** (pl. **badu**), or if they are from major cities, they are called **madani** (pl. **mudun**). Some people are attributed to their ethnicities: **druuze** (Druze); **ghajar** or **nawar** (gypsy); **shiishaan** (Chechen); **sharkas** (Circassians); **akraad** (Kurdish), etc. Others are associated with their religious sects: **3alawi** (Alawite), **maaruuni** (Maronite), etc.

In Jordan, you can also face one more classification. Some people consider themselves Jordanians of Palestinian origin. These are the people who originally lived west of the river Jordan before 1948 and 1967 but were expelled after the establishment of the state of Israel. It is likely that people will describe someone as being Jordanian of Jordanian origin, or Jordanian of Palestinian origin.

Unit Three

عيلتي

3eylti

My family

In this unit, you will learn about:

- Words for family members
- Cultural awareness
- Numbers 1–10
- Days of the week
- Identifying the letters (د، ذ، ر، ز، س، ش، ص، ض)

The Arab family

Arabs usually take pride in showing strong commitment to their close families. Most Arab families have long traditions of being mutually dependent on each other. The old support the young and the young respect the old, this is how it traditionally goes. It is not uncommon to see extended families living in the same home. Based on economic and/or social factors, it is common to find infants, children, teenagers, adults and their parents all living in the same house. Many families, those who can afford to, build apartments for their married sons to keep them and their new families in the same building. Essentially, people of the same family live together in the same house. This results in a complicated net of relationships. The father is the patriarch,

Table 3.1 Family members **(Audio 1.24–1.25)**

	Member	Meaning	Notes
1	`abu; `waalid; `baaba,	father	
2	`umm; imm; `waaldih; `maama	mother	
3	**ax**	brother	
4	**uxt**	sister	
5	**jadd; jidd; siid**	grandfather	
6	**jaddah; jiddih; sitt**	grandmother	
7	**3amm**	paternal uncle	
8	**3ammah; 3ammih**	paternal aunt	
9	**xaal**	maternal uncle	
10	**xaalah; xaalih**	maternal aunt	
11	**ibin; walad**	son; boy	
12	**bint**	daughter; girl	
13	**nasiib; nsiib; sihr**	in-law	
14	**Hama**	father in-law	
15	**Hamaah; Hamaat**	mother in-law	
16	**ibin 3amm**	male cousin	on the father's side
17	**binit 3amm/bint 3amm**	female cousin	on the father's side
18	**ibin xaal**	male cousin	on the mother's side
19	**binit xaal/bint xaal**	female cousin	on the mother's side
20	**zooj/jooz**	husband	
21	**zawjih/marah-**	wife	
22	**garaabah/garaabih**	relative	

everybody else lives under his leadership. Reality can be reflected in this description but can also deviate a little, and has indeed been changing slowly in recent years. Newly formed families are more independent and have a lot fewer members. Increasingly, the concept of the *family home* is diminishing due to education, work and economic factors. The patriarch can no longer afford to provide food and sustenance to all of the extended family members. Younger members of the same family are going after job opportunities outside of their traditional homes, women are increasingly joining the workforce, the age of marriage is nearing the 30s even for women, and family size is getting smaller and smaller. Yet, family values are still respected. All members of the family still show great respect for *the father of the house.*

 Dialogue 1 (Audio 1.26–1.27)

 Emad and Samir are sitting in a café. Emad is browsing his photo gallery on his cellphone, showing his family members to Samir.

3IMAAD: shuuf ya samiir, haay ummi, wa haadh abuuy.
SAMIIR: maa shaa allaah! w miin haay?
3IMAAD: haay uxti iSSaghiirih, isimha manaar.
SAMIIR: Hilwah kthiir. w haadha miin?
3IMAAD: haadha axuuy likabiir 3umar
SAMIIR: 3eilih raaʔiʕah!
3IMAAD: intah arwa3

EMAD: *Look Samir, this is my mother, and this is my father.*
SAMIR: *Great! And who is this?*
EMAD: *This is my little sister, her name is Manar.*
SAMIR: *So beautiful. And who is this?*
EMAD: *This is my older brother, Omar.*
SAMIR: *Very nice family!*
EMAD: *You're even better.*

Vocabulary

shuuf (sh+w+f)	look! (masc. sing.)
miin	who?
haay	this is (when referring to fem. sing.)
haadha	this is (when referring to masc. sing.)
maa shaa allaah	This is great!
Saghiir (S+gh+r)	small; young
kabiir (k+b+r)	big; old
Hilu (masc.); Hilwah (fem.)	good-looking; pretty
kthiir (k+th+r)	a lot
raaʔiɜ (r+w+ɜ)	wonderful (**raaʔiɜah** [fem.])

New expressions

maa shaa allaah: lit., whatever God wanted! This expression is loaded. It can change meanings based on context and intonation. Here, it is an expression of gratitude to God for something good. So, if someone is telling you about a beautiful place, or about a success story, a brilliant person, etc., you can respond by saying *maa shaa allaah!* It can also be used to express discontent about something you really do not like. For example, if someone is doing something that is way below expectations, you can say *maa shaa allaah!* to express that you're not happy with it. The context usually decides the meaning.

You just saw a very handsome kid. You comment saying:

> **maa shaa allaah. ilwalad Hilu.**
> Wow! The kid is very handsome.

Dialogue 2 (Audio 1.28–1.29)

Emad has invited an American exchange student, Mark, to his home for a Ramadan dinner. He is introducing Mark to his family.

3IMAAD: it`faDDal ya maark; ahlan wa sahlan.
MAARK: ahlan biik.
3IMAAD: mumkin a3arrfak 3ala 3eilti? haadha jiddi, wa haay jidditi
MAARK: tsharrafna.
3IMAAD: wa haadha 3ammi abu xaalid, wa 3ammti um xaalid.
MAARK: ahlan wa sahlan.
3IMAAD: kamaan haadha xaali abu aHmad, wa xaalti umm aHmad.
MAARK: ahleyn.

EMAD: *Come in, Mark; welcome!*
MARK: *Welcome to you, too.*
EMAD: *May I introduce you to my family? This is my grandfather,*
        and this is my grandmother.
MARK: *I'm honored.*
EMAD: *And this is my uncle Abu Khalid, and my aunt Um Khalid.*
MARK: *Hello!*
EMAD: *And this is my uncle Abu Ahmad and my aunt Um Ahmad.*
MARK: *Welcome.*

Vocabulary

mumkin   possible (is it possible?)

a3arrfak 3ala (3+r+r+f)   to introduce someone to

3eilti (3eilih+i)   family + my (my family)

Exercise 1a

Using the information from Table 3.1, read the following paragraph then answer the questions that follow.

yuusif is married to samiira. He has one brother named SaaliH and one sister named manaal. He also has two children: Sabri and waa?il. His father's name is mHammad, and his mother's name is muna. ibrahiim is samiira's father and imaan is her mother. samiira has another sister named wafaa? and a brother named 3abdallah.

Match the names in Arabic to their English counterpart. Use the transliteration key for help.

Arabic	English	Arabic	English
1 منى	yuusif	7 محمد	mHammad
2 وائل	samiira	8 يوسف	muna
3 عبدالله	SaaliH	9 منال	ibrahiim
4 ابراهيم	manaal	10 صالح	imaan
5 وفاء	Sabri	11 صبري	wafaa?
6 سميرة	waa?il	12 ايمان	3abdallah

Exercise 1b

Using the paragraph above, fill in the blanks in each of the following and provide the translation.

e.g., **samiira zawjit[1] yuusif**
Samira is Yousef's wife

1 Sabri _____ waa?il
2 samiira _____ wafaa?
3 ibrahiim _____ yuusif
4 imaan _____ samiira
5 mHammad _____ samiira
6 mHammad _____ muna
7 manaal _____ Sabri
8 muna _____ SaliH
9 Sabri _____ yuusif
10 wafaa? _____ waa?il
11 yuusif _____ samiira
12 SaaliH _____ mHammad

1 The feminine marker /**-ah**/ or /**-ih**/ changes to /**-at**/ or /**-it**/ if the word is first part of the IDaafah construct. This construct will be explained soon.

Numbers 1–10

Learning numbers is very helpful in any language. It is instrumental in talking about one's age, giving directions, negotiating or telling the time and, in Arabic, saying most days of the week. Numbers are pronounced a little differently in LA and MSA. Table 3.2 shows the numbers 1–10. In LA, the question word most commonly used to ask about numbers is /**kam**/, meaning how much or how many.

Table 3.2 Numbers 1–10 **(Audio 1.30)**

Number		LA	MSA
1	١	waaHad; waaHid	waaHid
2	٢	iththnein; thnein; tnein	iththnaan
3	٣	thalaathah; thalaathih; talaatah; talaatih	thalaath
4	٤	arba3ah	arba3ah
5	٥	xamsah; xamsih	xamsah
6	٦	sittah; sittih	sittah
7	٧	sab3ah	sab3ah
8	٨	thamaanyah; tamaanyih	thamaanyah
9	٩	tis3ah	tis3ah
10	١٠	3asharah	3asharah

Countable nouns are by default singular. If you want to specify number with a singular noun, you can write the noun followed by the number. In this case, both the noun and the number must agree in gender; see the examples below. Arabic is provided so that you can observe the feminine marker.

Examples: **(Audio 1.31–1.32)**

1A:	**ktaab**	كتاب	a book
1B:	**ktaab waaHid/ktaab waaHad**	كتاب واحد	one book
2A:	**sayyaarah**	سيّارة	a car
2B:	**sayyaarah waHdih**	سيارة واحدة	one car

For the number two, most speakers in LA would simply add the suffix /-**eyn**/ to the singular noun to denote the dual. Rarely do people use the number "two" the way presented for "one" in 1B and 2B.

Examples:

3A:	**ktaabeyn**	كتابين	two books
3B:	**ktaabeyn iththneyn**	كتابين اثنين	two books
4A:	**sayyaarteyn**	سيّارتين	two cars
4B:	**sayyaarteyn thinteyn**	سيّارتين ثنتين	two cars

When using numbers from 3 to 10, the number is mentioned first, then the countable nouns in the plural form. The suffix /-**ah**/ or /-**ih**/ is deleted.

Examples:

5:	**thalaath kutub**	ثلاث كُتُب	three books
6:	**xams sayyaraat**	خَمس سيّارات	five cars
7:	**sabi3 muhandisaat**	سَبِع مُهندسات	seven engineers (fem.)
8:	**arba3 Tullaab**	أربع طلاب	four students (masc.)
9:	**3ashr glaam**	عشر أقلام	ten pens
10:	**sitt banaat**	ستّ بنات	six girls

Exercise 2

Say and write the following in LA; use the vocabulary introduced in previous units.

1 Five guys
2 Two doors
3 One summer
4 Ten teachers (masc.)
5 Six teachers (fem.)

Exercise 3

Translate each of the following statements into English. Try to guess the meaning of the particles.

1 kam ax 3indak?
2 kam galam ma3ik?
3 kam bint fi ilbeyt?
4 kam walad kabiir?
5 kam binit raa?3ah?

Exercise 4

Ask questions that would provide the given answers.

1 xams shabaab
2 ktaab waaHad
3 qalameyn
4 thalaath muhandisiin
5 3ashr dolaraat

Following are ordinal numbers from 1–10. These are adjectives; there-fore, I will present the masculine and feminine forms. Keep in mind that in Arabic, adjectives follow the nouns they modify.

Table 3.3 Ordinal numbers **(Audio 1.33)**

Number		LA (masc.)	LA (fem.)	MSA (masc.)	MSA (fem.)
1	١	?awwal	?uula	?awwal	?uula
2	٢	thaani; taani	thaanyih; taanyih	thaani	thaaniyah
3	٣	thaalith; taalit	thaalthih; taaltih	thaalith	thaalithah
4	٤	raabi3	raab3ah; raab3ih	raabi3	raabi3ah
5	٥	xaamis	xaamsih	xaamis	xaamisah
6	٦	saadis	saadsih	saadis	saadisah
7	٧	saabi3	saab3ah; saab3ih	saabi3	saabi3ah
8	٨	thaamin; taamin	thaamnih; taamnih	thaamin	thaaminah
9	٩	taasi3	taas3ah; taas3ih	taasi3	taasi3ah
10	١٠	3aashir	3aashrih	3aashir	3aashirah

Exercise 5

Say and write (using transliteration) the following in LA:

1 First book
2 Second car
3 Tenth student
4 Third summer
5 Eighth teacher

Days of the week (Audio 1.34)

Days of the week in Arabic are in line with numbers except for two of them. Generally, days of the week come with the definite article /**il-**/. Review the rules for the definite article and see when assimilation takes place. Table 3.4 presents the days of the week.

Table 3.4 Days of the week

LA	MSA	English	Notes
ilaHad	alaHad	Sunday	same root as **waaHad; waaHid**
iththneyn	aliththneyn	Monday	same root as **thneyn; iththnaan**
iththalaatha	aththulaathaa	Tuesday	same root as **thalaathah; thalaathih**
ilarba3a	alarbu3aa	Wednesday	same root as **arba3ah**
ilxamiis	alxamiis	Thursday	same root as **xamsah; xamsih**
iljumm3ah	aljumu3ah	Friday	the day of "gathering"
issabt; issabit	assabt	Saturday	Sabbath

As you can see, days of the week are in line with numbers except for two of them: Friday is traditionally a holiday in the Arab/Muslim world. It is the day when people meet (**j**, **m**, **3** has the root meaning of *to get together*). This day's name is derived from the Friday noon prayers which are commonly attended by most Muslims. The word for Saturday is obviously similar to that used in Hebrew.

Finally, the definite article attached to these days is dropped mostly when one wants to express an event that recurs on a given day, for example, **kull xamiis**: every Thursday.

Dialogue 3 (Audio 1.35–1.36)

John, an exchange student, is talking to his classmate, Amir, about his weekly schedule.

3AAMIR:	marHaba joon, shuu 3indak ilyoom?
JOON:	alhan 3aamir. ilyoom ilaHad 3indi dars ?adab 3arabi.
3AAMIR:	kwayyis. wa bukrah?
JOON:	bukrah iththneyn fiih 3indi dars 3arabi kamaan, wa riyaaDah.
3AAMIR:	iththalaatha ?akiid ma 3indak Saff.
JOON:	SaHiiH, iththalaatha 3uTlah.
3AAMIR:	wa yoom ilarba3a?
JOON:	ilarba3a wa ilxamiis laazim adrus fi ilmaktabih kull ilyoom.
3AAMIR:	mumtaaz.
JOON:	wa iljumm3ah maa fiih ishi.

AMIR:	*Hello John, what do you have today?*
JOHN:	*Hello Amir, today, Sunday, I have a lesson on Arabic literature.*
AMIR:	*Good. Tomorrow?*
JOHN:	*Tomorrow, Monday, I have a lesson on Arabic too, and sports.*
AMIR:	*Tuesday you certainly do not have a class.*
JOHN:	*Right, Tuesday is a break.*
AMIR:	*And Wednesday?*
JOHN:	*Wednesday and Thursday, I have to study in the library for the whole day.*
AMIR:	*Excellent.*
JOHN:	*And on Friday, there is nothing.*

Vocabulary

shuu	what
dars (d+r+s)	lesson
?adab (?+d+b)	literature
bukrah (b+k+r)	tomorrow
yoom (y+w+m)	day
fiih	in/there is/there are/there (*exists*)
riyaaDah (r+y+D)	sports
?akiid (a+k+d)	certainly
Saff (S+f+f)	class
SaHiiH (S+H+H)	right
mumtaaz	excellent
3uTlah (3+T+T+l)	vacation; day off; break
?ayaam	days
kull	every
?awwal (a+w+l)	first
?aaxir (a+x+r)	last
shaari3	street
maktab (k+t+b):	office
maktabah	library
miin	who?
ma; maa	what?

Exercise 6

Based on Dialogue 3 above, write the days when John does each of the following activities:

1 Sports
2 Arabic literature
3 Day off
4 Study at the library
5 Arabic lesson
6 Weekend

Identifying the letters ض ،ص ،ش ،س ،ز ،ر ،ذ ،د

Exercise 7

Write each of the following letters three times:

د	س
ذ	ش
ر	ص
ز	ض

Exercise 8 (Bonus audio 4)

Join the following letters to make up words. Add short vowels where appropriate (where they appear on the letters in isolation). Refer to the transliteration key if you need help. Again, make sure you start from right to left. Practise reading the words aloud.

1 دُ ب (bear)
2 ذ ي ب (wolf)
3 حُ و رُ (spirit)
4 ز ي ت (oil)
5 س حَ ا ب (zipper)
6 شِ رّ ي ر (evil)
7 ص ا ح ب (friend; owner of)
8 ضَ ر ي ر (blind)
9 نِ سِ ر (eagle)
10 حَ ا رّ (hot)

Exercise 9

Identify the letters (ض ،ص ،ش ،س ،ز ،ر ،ذ ،د) in the following paragraph. There is no need to worry about the letters you do not know at this time.

د	ذ	ر	ز	س	ش	ص	ض

العراق دولة تقع في شمال غرب العالم العربي. يبلغ عدد سكان العراق حوالي
ستة و ثلاثين مليون نسمة. يحدّه من الشمال تركيا، و من الغرب إيران، من

الجنوب الكويت و السعودية ومن الشرق سوريا و الأردن. تعتبر دولة العراق
واحدة من أقدم الحضارات في العالم. فقد قامت حضارة ما بين بلاد الرافدين قبل
أكثر من ثمانية آلاف سنة، و في العراق تم اختراع الكتابة المسمارية و كان
السومريون من أول الشعوب التي حكمت هذه البلاد. و كانت العراق أيضاً مهداً
للحضارة الاكادية، و الآشورية و البابلية. و بعد ظهور الإسلام انتقلت عاصمة
الدولة الإسلامية اليها في زمن الدولة العباسية. من أهم مدنها بغداد، الموصل،
كربلاء، و البصرة في الجنوب.

 ## Cultural point

Understanding relationships within the typical Arab family can be very informative. Here are some general practices. Some of these practices can slightly differ from one place to another.

- It is not uncommon for adults above the age of 18 to continue to live with their families and depend on them. This is especially true in the case of students and girls. Generally, girls stay in the same home as their parents until they get married.
- Housekeeping and cooking are mostly the work of females: mothers and sisters. You can see everyone at lunch or dinner having a great time. Then once the eating part is over, the mother and sisters work to clean up, do the washing up and prepare some tea for the men who sit together enjoying a movie or watching a soccer game.
- In the presence of guests, some families prefer having two living areas: one for males and one for females. Other families are fine having everyone in the same room.
- Food etiquette is important but it will be discussed in detail in subsequent units.
- The heavy presence of communication technology – cell phones and handheld devices – is contributing to an ongoing change in family relations. It is now more common to see people sitting in the same place hooked up to their devices. Arabs are still trying to define proper behavior when using these devices in public.

Unit Four

مش عارِف
mish 3aarif

I do not know!

In this unit, you will learn about:

- Asking questions
- Cultural awareness
- Questions: yes/no
- Questions: who; what; where; when; how much/many
- Negation with **ma**, **mish**, **laa** . . .
- High frequency propositions
- Nominal and verbal sentences: introduction
- Identifying the letters (ط، ظ، ع، غ، ف، ق، ك، ل)

Yes/no questions

Two elements are usually present when asking questions in most languages: the question word and intonation. There are different types of questions: yes/no questions, information or wh- questions and tag questions. In LA, all of these three types utilize one major form of intonation; that is, all questions have very similar pitch. Intonation generally refers to pitch variation: the fact that different utterances have different beats, or different *music*. Think of how informative/ declarative statements versus questions are pronounced. LA mostly utilizes pitch variation to form a yes/no question. But a question word is used to form the equivalent of a wh- question besides utilizing intonation, of course. One other thing is that Arabic does not require a change of word order when forming a question. English, for example, requires subject/verb inversion. One thing to keep in mind is that in all units to come in this book, all yes/no questions will be marked in writing using only the addition of the question mark. Keep in mind that yes/no questions in Arabic require no changes in writing from statements, therefore; the only marker in writing is the question mark. See Table 4.1.

Table 4.1 Yes/no questions **(Audio 1.37; Bonus audio 8)**

	Yes/no question	Translation	Response	Translation
1	**intah urduni?**	Are you Jordanian?	**aywah, ana urduni**	Yes, I am Jordanian
2	**inti faransiyyih?**	Are you French?	**la, ana mish faransiyyih, ana amrikiyyih**	No, I'm not French, I'm American
3	**xaalid muhandis?**	Is Khalid an engineer?	**la, xaalid duktoor**	No, Khalid is a doctor
4	**ma3ak diinaar?**	Do you have one dinar?	**aah, tfaDDal**	Yes, there you go (you can have it)

Notice that the sentence structure does not change at all in Arabic. The only, but very important, change is that of intonation.

Wh- questions

The only addition to these types of questions is the question word.
Wh- questions maintain the same intonation patterns of questions
and do not require changes in word order. It is important to notice
how these questions are answered. Later in the book, more advanced
answers will be presented. Table 4.2 presents some information
questions.

Table 4.2 Information questions

Information question	Translation	Response	Translation
1	**miin daras 3arabi?**	Who studied Arabic?	**xaalid daras 3arabi.**	Khalid studied Arabic.
2	**shuu/eish ismak?**	What's your name?	**ismi xaalid.**	My name is Khalid.
3	**weyn leyla?**	Where's Laila?	**leyla fi iljaam3ah.**	Laila is at the university.
4	**mata/eimta/ ameit saafar xaalid**	When did Khalid leave?	**xaalid saafar ams/imbaariH.**	Khalid left yesterday.
	bikam haay ilsayyaarah?	How much is this car?	**bi 3ashar alaaf diinaar.**	It's ten thousand dinars.

Negation with maa, mish, muu and laa

These markers are very commonly used in LA to form negations. The
first one, /**maa**/ or /**ma**/, negates verbs and prepositional phrases.
The second one, /**mish**/, negates adjectives and demonstratives.
/**mish**/ and /**muu**/ are almost identical, except that /**muu**/ is more
representative of Syrian dialect. /**laa**/ or /**la**/ simply means "no." It
can be used as a short answer to a yes/no question. However, it is
often followed by another negation statement to emphasize the
answer. Sometimes, the suffix /**-ish**/ is added to the end of the verb
or prepositional phrase negated by /**maa**/. See Table 4.3.

Table 4.3 Negation with **maa**, **mish**, **muu** and **laa** (**Audio 1.38**)

Yes/no question	Response with negation	Notes
ma3ak ktaab?	la, maa ma3i ktaab la, ma ma3iish ktaab la, ma3iish ktaab	Mostly stylistic differences between the three responses. Meaning is the same.
xaalid daras 3arabi?	la, xaalid ma daras 3arabi la, xaalid ma darasish 3arabi xaalid ma darasish 3arabi	
intah mabsuuT?	la, ana mish mabsuuT la, ana muu mabsuuT	
xaalid w salma raaHu 3ala irbid?	la, ma raaHuush 3ala irbid la, ma raaHu 3ala irbid	
inti amriikiyyih?	la, ana mish amriikiyyih la, ana muu amriikiyyih	
3indak sayyaarah?	la, ma 3indi sayyaarah la ma 3indiish sayyaarah ma 3indiish sayyaarah	

Dialogue 1 (Audio 1.39–1.40)

Sami is calling his friend, Khalid. They both want to go have
breakfast.

SAAMI:	aluu, marHaba xaalid, keyfak?
XAALID:	ahlan wa sahlan saami. ana mabsuuT.
SAAMI:	ahlan biik. ʔafTarit?
XAALID:	la, maa ʔafTarit. biddak tifTir?
SAAMI:	aywah, weyn?
XAALID:	mumkin fi maT3am ilbalad.
SAAMI:	tamaam, mata?
XAALID:	ba3d saa3ah, kwayyis?
SAAMI:	kwayyis, bass weyn haadha ilmaT3am?
XAALID:	ʔaaxir shaari3 iljaam3ah.

SAAMI: aah, maashi, bashuufak hnaak.
XAALID: maashi, ma3 issalaamih.
SAAMI: ma3 issalaamih.

SAMI: *Hello, hi Khalid, how are you?*
KHALID: *Welcome, Sami.*
SAMI: *Welcome to you, too. Have you had breakfast?*
KHALID: *No, I have not. Would you like to have breakfast?*
SAMI: *Yes, where?*
KHALID: *Maybe at Albalad restaurant.*
SAMI: *Fine, when?*
KHALID: *In an hour, is that good?*
SAMI: *Good, but where is this restaurant?*
KHALID: *End of the University Street.*
SAMI: *Oh, OK, will see you there.*
KHALID: *OK, goodbye.*
SAMI: *Goodbye.*

Vocabulary

laa; la	no
maa; ma	no; not
mish	not
-iish	-not
mabsuuT (b+s+T)	happy
ʔafTarit (f+T+r)	to have breakfast
bidd+/badd+ak	like to; want to
tamaam (t+m+m)	fine; great; OK; wonderful
saa3ah (pl. saa3aat)	hour; watch
maT3am (T+3+m)	restaurant
aah	OK; I see
maashi (m+sh+y)	sure; OK (will do; agree)
hnaak/hunaak/hinaak	there
ma3 issalaamih (s+l+m)	goodbye (lit. with safety)

New expressions

tamaam: lit., full; complete. This word is used extensively to express that one is happy, or something is going well.

> **iljaw ilyoom tamaam, kthiir Hilu.**
> The weather today is perfect, very nice.

aah: lit., yes. This word is used to express agreement, or to give an indication that you're following the details of a story, waiting to see how it will end.

> **mumkin truuH ma3i lil jaam3ah?**   **aah, mumkin.**
> Would you go with me to the university?   yes, I would.

maashi: lit., walking. Used to express agreement or say that you're fine (when asked how you're doing).

> **shuu ra?ykum nruuH 3al gahwih?**   **maashi, yallah.**
> What do you think of (us) going to the café?   Sure, let's go.

Exercise 1

Match the following questions with the proper answers:

Question	Response	Answers
1 weyn ilmaktabih?	a bi diinaar waaHid bass	1 _____
2 mata saafarti 3ala irbid?	b imbaariH	2 _____
3 miin afTar fi ilmaT3am?	c saa3ah min maama	3 _____
4 bikam haadha liktaab?	d aHmad wa xaalid wa salma	4 _____
5 shuu haay?	e fi iljaam3ah	5 _____

Exercise 2

In the following lists of words, mark the odd one out.

1 weyn	miin	bikam	haadha
2 sayyaarah	ktaab	dars	maktabih
3 tamaam	ahlan	kwayyis	maashi
4 ma3	shuu	ba3d	3ind
5 mish	laa	fi	maa

Dialogue 2 (Audio 1.41)

Salma is home. Her mother, who is out, is calling to ask if she made lunch.

SALMA: aluu, kiifik maama?
MOTHER: hala maama, ana kwaysih. initi kiifik?
SALMA: kull shi tamaam.
MOTHER: 3milti ghada?
SALMA: ma 3milit ghada, mata btiSalu ilbeyt?
MOTHER: ba3d saa3tein.
SALMA: maashi, halla? ba3mal ghada.
MOTHER: shukran yaa maama.
SALMA: allaah ysallmik, maama.

SALMA: *Hello, How are you mom?*
MOTHER: *Hello mom,[1] I'm good, how are you?*
SALMA: *Everything is OK.*
MOTHER: *Have you made lunch?*
SALMA: *I haven't made lunch, when are you arriving home?*
MOTHER: *In two hours.*
SALMA: *OK, now I will make lunch.*
MOTHER: *Thank you mom.*
SALMA: *May God protect you, mom.*

1 Notice that in Arab culture, a mother might call her kids using /**maama**/ and a father does the same using /**baaba**/.

Vocabulary

hala	welcome; more endearment than "ahleyn"
3milti (3+m+l)	to do; to make
ghada	lunch
btiSalu (w+S+l)	to arrive
halla?	now; soon
ysallmik (s+l+m)	to protect: to save

Exercise 3

Fill in the blanks using the correct negation particle (maa, mish, muu, laa). Translations are provided.

1 obaama _____ muslim.   Obama is not Muslim.
2 liktaab _____ ma3i.   The book is not with me.
3 _____ katabit iddars ilyoom.   I have not written the lesson today.
4 _____, maa 3indi bint.   No, I do not have a daughter.
5 _____ ruHt 3ala ilbattra.   I have not visited Petra.

High frequency prepositions

Prepositions do not have fixed meanings. The best way to learn them is to understand their general usages and practice them in different contexts. Table 4.3 presents the most commonly used prepositions in LA.

Table 4.3 High frequency prepositions

	LA	English	Notes
1	**bi** بِ	with	Usually contracted to b.
2	**min** مِن	from	Used to specify a beginning point in time or place.
3	**li** لِ **il** إلـ **la** لـ	to	Mostly used to express possessiveness; sometimes used instead of **ila** to express end point in time or place. Do not confuse this with the definite article.
4	**3an** عَن	about	
5	**3ala** علَى	on, over	
6	**fi** في	in	Compare to /**fii**/ which means "there is" or "there are."

In Arabic writing, the prepositions in 1 and 3 connect to the noun they precede. Others are written as separate words. Consider the following examples:

1	خالد بالبيت	**xaalid bilbeyt**
		Khalid is at home
2	الشاي بنص دينار	**ishshay bnuSS diinaar**
		The tea is half a dinar
3	من الوحدة للخمسة	**min ilwaHdih lilxamsih**
		From 1:00 to 5:00
4	بدي أنام للأربعة	**biddi anaam lilarba3ah**
		I want to sleep till 4:00
5	هاي السيارة إلك؟	**haay issayyaarah ilak?**
		Is this car yours?
6	تامر بحكي عنها	**taamir biHki 3anha**
		Tamir talks about her
7	الكتاب على الطاولة	**ilktaab 3aTTaawlih**
		The book is on the table
8	السيارة في الكراج	**issayyaarah filkaraaj**
		The car is in the garage

Exercise 4

Fill in the blanks with the correct preposition

1 salma raaHat _____ iljaam3ah.
2 madiinat ilbatra _____ ilurdun.
3 ilkoola (Coke) _____ diinar.
4 ana badrus _____ issaa3ah thalaath _____ issaa3ah
 thamaanyih.
5 haada ittalifoon _____ ummi.

Nominal and verbal sentences: introduction

Sentences are of two main types: nominal and verbal. A nominal
sentence is one that starts with a noun or a pronoun. A verbal
sentence starts with a verb. A nominal sentence can either have a
verb or only have a subject and predicate. If the sentence has a verb,
there has to be a subject associated with it. The subject can either
be pronounced (either a noun or a pronoun) or embedded (i.e., the
subject is understood). As mentioned previously, word order in LA is
not so strict, as long as the sentence starts with a definite noun or
with a verb that has a subject. Usually, sentences start with a subject;

however, they also can start with a verb. It is important to understand sentence build-up in LA. This is an accumulative process but we can begin looking at it. Table 4.4 shows examples of simple nominal and verbal sentences in LA. Sentence units are labeled.

Table 4.4 Nominal and verbal sentences in LA **(Audio 1.42)**

	LA	LA (sentence units labeled)	English
1	**il+beyt kbiir**	the+house big	The house is big.
2	**xaalid mabsuuT**	Khalid happy	Khalid is happy.
3	**salma muhandis+ih**	Salma engineer+fem.	Salma is an engineer.
4	**3ind+i sayyaarah**	with+me car	I have a car.
5	**ma3+i ktaab mumtaaz**	with+me book excellent	I have an excellent book.
6	**afTar+t fi il+beyt il+yoom**	had breakfast+I at the home today	I had breakfast at home today.
7	**daras xaalid fi il+maktabih**	study Khalid at the library	Khalid studied at the library.
8	**raaH 3ala il+jaam3ah**	went to the+university	He went to the university.
9	**raaH+at 3ala is+suug**	went+she to the+souk	She went to the souk.
10	**3mil+na ghada**	made+we lunch	We made/prepared lunch.

Notice the following: in the present tense, there is no verb "to be" as in English; sentences 2 and 3 start with proper names; sentences 4 and 5 start with prepositions that have a possessive pronoun; and sentences 6–10 all start with verbs that have defined subjects.

Exercise 5

Use the list of vocabulary in the following box to make ten short nominal and verbal sentences.

shabaab	ʔaruuH	ma3ak	ismii	Hilu	raaʔi3
raaʔi3ah	3eilti	ilʔadab	iSSaff	saHiiH	mumtaaz
3uTlah	katab	issaa3ah	ilmaT3am	ʔafTarit	

Identifying the letters ل ،ك ،ق ،ف ،غ ،ع ،ظ ،ط

Exercise 6

Write each of the following letters 3 times:

ط ف

ظ ق

ع ك

غ ل

Exercise 7 **(Bonus audio 9)**

Join the following letters to make up a word. Add short vowels where appropriate (where they appear on the letters in isolation). Refer to the transliteration key if you need help. Again, make sure you start from right to left. Practise reading the words aloud.

1 ط َ ل ب (he asked; requested)

2 ظ َ ر ف (envelope; condition)

3 ع َ ر َ ب ي (Arab; an Arab)

4 غ َ ز ا ل (deer)

5 ف ي ل (elephant)

6 ق َ ل ب (heart)

7 ك ا س (cup)

8 ل و ز (almond)

9 ف َ ر ي د (unique)

10 ط َ ل ع (he left)

Exercise 8

Identify the letters (ل ،ك ،ق ،ف ،غ ،ع ،ظ ،ط) in the following paragraph. There is no need to worry about the letters you do not know at this time.

ل	ك	ق	ف	غ	ع	ظ	ط

العراق دولة تقع في شمال غرب العالم العربي. يبلغ عدد سكان العراق حوالي
ستة و ثلاثين مليون نسمة. يحدّه من الشمال تركيا، و من الغرب إيران، من

الجنوب الكويت و السعودية ومن الشرق سوريا و الأردن. تعتبر دولة العراق
واحدة من أقدم الحضارات في العالم. فقد قامت حضارة ما بين بلاد الرافدين قبل
أكثر من ثمانية آلاف سنة، و في العراق تم اختراع الكتابة المسمارية و كان
السومريون من أول الشعوب التي حكمت هذه البلاد. و كانت العراق أيضاً مهداً
للحضارة الاكادية، و الآشورية و البابلية. و بعد ظهور الإسلام انتقلت عاصمة
الدولة الإسلامية اليها في زمن الدولة العباسية. من أهم مدنها بغداد، الموصل،
كربلاء، و البصرة في الجنوب.

 ## Cultural point

Asking is not particular to Arab culture. The questions asked can be particular. Matters of life that are deemed private in Western culture can be less private in Arab culture, which makes them possible targets of questions. These include asking about one's job, family, income, marital status, religious affiliation and religious beliefs. Some people follow up with further questions and discussion, especially when religious beliefs and political views are different from their own. The best way to go about this is to give very general and much less provoking answers and try to end the discussion politely by changing the subject. In most cases, there will be someone who is familiar with different cultures. If so, make sure to ask for his/her help or to indicate that you would like to avoid such questions and discussions.

Some people go as far as trying to convert you to Islam. In principle, this is a very common practice in Christianity and in Islam. Some churches and some Muslim scholars embark on major efforts to invite people to their religions. Some individuals like to take on this endeavor. It is up to you to engage in discussions of this sort or to simply promise to read and follow things up on your own. If you end up discussing religion in the Arab world, you should keep in mind that most Arabs (Muslims and Christians alike) believe in the existence of God, so challenging this might bring up some debate. My personal experience is that avoiding issues of religious, racial and political divides saves a lot of time for learning language. There will be much more chance for these types of engagements at more advanced levels of language proficiency.

Unit Five

فلافل و كباب

falaafil wa kabaab

Falafel and kebab

In this unit, you will learn about:

- Ordering in a restaurant
- Food etiquette
- Jordanian currency
- Telling the time
- Numbers – extension
- Countable nouns
- Identifying the letters (م، ن، هـ، و، لا، ي)

Dining at restaurants

Dining out requires understanding of food culture in the Arab world. Major cities are abundant with different kinds of restaurants serving different types of food. As is the case in other parts of the world, restaurants in the Arab world have a lot in common and also have some differences. Fast food restaurants serve local foods, mostly sandwiches, pastries and a number of main dishes. These include falafel and shawarma sandwiches. Shawarma is slices of beef, lamb or chicken wrapped in pita bread with some sauce, spices, pickles, tomatoes and lettuce. The individual recipes can, of course, vary a little from one place to another. Main dishes usually include rice and chicken, beef or lamb in some kind of stew. Grilled meat (**mashaawi**) restaurants are also common. They serve kebabs, chicken, beef or lamb skewers and a long list of mezzes.

Western fast food chains – McDonald's, Pizza Hut, Burger King, etc. – are also available in most major cities in the Arab world. Foods served here are pretty much similar to their mother branches but you will find some changes to conform with local cultures.

Tips are only common in upscale restaurants. Most non-tourist restaurants do not expect you to tip their servers but if you do, it is usually a very good gesture. Another difference is that leftovers are usually not carried out. However, this practice has been changing recently. In most restaurants now, people can ask for boxes to take away their food leftovers.

Most restaurants, excluding upscale tourist ones, do not serve desserts. They just serve main dishes, salads and soft drinks along with tea and Turkish coffee. Instead, desserts have their specific places where you can find different sorts of Arabic sweets and ice creams.

Dialogue 1 (Audio 1.43–1.44)

Samir is in a restaurant for breakfast. He is discussing his options with the waiter.

SAAMIR: marHaba abu ishshabaab.
GARSOON: ahleyn. tfaDDal.
SAAMIR: biddi SaHin HummuS wa SaHin fuul wa 3ashar Habbaat falaafil.
GARSOON: tikram. shay, qahwah, bibsi, mayyih?
SAAMIR: shay law samaHt, sukkar zyaadih.
GARSOON: HaaDir.
The waiter brings the plates.
GARSOON: tfaDDal, ay shi thaani?
SAAMIR: la, shukran.
Samir is done and wants to pay.
SAAMIR: liHsaab law samaHt.
GARSOON: tfaDDal, thalaath dananiir.
SAAMIR: haay thalaath dananiir.
GARSOON: SiHteyn.
SAAMIR: 3ala galbak.

SAMIR: *Hello, buddy.*
WAITER: *Hello, what can I do for you?*
SAMIR: *I want a hummus plate, a fava bean plate and ten pieces of falafel.*
WAITER: *With pleasure. Tea, coffee, Pepsi, water?*
SAMIR: *Tea, if you don't mind, with extra sugar.*
WAITER: *Done!*
The waiter brings the plates.
WAITER: *There you go, anything else?*
SAMIR: *No, thanks.*
Samir is done and wants to pay.
SAMIR: *The check, please.*
WAITER: *There you go, three dinars.*
SAMIR: *This is it, three dinars.*
WAITER: *With much health.*
SAMIR: *Health with your heart.*

Vocabulary

garSoon	waiter
abu ishshabaab	buddy
SaHin	plate; dish
HummuS	hummus
fuul	fava beans
Habbah; Habbih (pl. Habbaat)	piece, pieces
falaafil	falafel
tikram (k+r+m)	with all generosity
shay	tea
gahwah (ʔahwih)	coffee
bibsi	Pepsi (could be used for any cola drink product)
mayyih; may	water
law samaHt (s+m+H)	please, if you wish
sukkar	sugar
zyaadih (z+y+d)	extra
HaaDir (H+D+r)	sure; will do
tfaDDal? (f+D+l)	how can I help you?
ay	any
shi	thing
thaani	second; else; other; another
Hsaab (H+s+b)	check
dinaar (pl. dananiir)	dinar; dinars
SiHteyn	with health
3ala galbak	same to you (lit. to your heart)

Dialogue 2 (Audio 1.45–1.47)

Three people, Mark, Salma and Laila, are at a restaurant having dinner.

GARSOON:	ahlan shabaab. shuu bitu?muru?
MAARK:	mumkin ilminyu law samaHt?
GARSOON:	bi3yuuni, tfaDDal.
SALMA:	ana biddi waaHad mashaawi mshakkal.
GARSOON:	HaaDir, madaam.
LEYLA:	shuu 3indkum salaTaat w muqabilaat?
GARSOON:	fiih HummuS, mtabbal, salaTah Haarrah, mHammarah, kibbih, laban, falaafil w mxlallalaat.
LEYLA:	mumkin waaHad mtabbal, w talaatih kiibih, w SaHin mxallal.
GARSOON:	taHit amrik.
MAARK:	wa ana biddi SaHin sheysh jaaj, w SaHin mHammarah.
GARSOON:	HaaDir. 3ashar dagaayig.

WAITER:	*Welcome guys. What can I do for you?*
MARK:	*Can we have the menu, please?*
WAITER:	*Sure, there you go.*
SALMA:	*I want a plate of mixed grill.*
WAITER:	*Sure, madam.*
LAILA:	*What salads and appetizers do you have?*
WAITER:	*We have hummus, babaganoush, spicy salad, hot pepper dip, meat-stuffed bulgur, yogurt, falafel and pickles.*
LAILA:	*May I have babaganoush, three pieces of meat-stuffed bulgur and a plate of pickles?*
WAITER:	*At your disposal.*
MARK:	*And I want a plate of chicken shesh and a plate of hot pepper dip.*
WAITER:	*Will be ready in ten minutes.*

(Audio 1.48; Bonus audio 12)

Vocabulary

bi+tu?muru (a+m+r)	to order; what do you order
il+minyu	the menu
bi+3yuun+i (3eyn; pl. 3yuun)	sure (lit. with my eyes)
mashaawi (sh+w+a)	grilled meat
mshakkal (sh+k+k+l)	mixed
salaTah (pl. salaTaat)	salad
muqabilaat (no sing. form)	appetizers
mtabbal	mashed zucchini; mashed eggplant
Haarrah	spicy; hot
mHammarah	mashed hot pepper
kibbih	meat-stuffed bulgur balls
laban	yogurt; sour cream
mxlallal; mxallalaat	pickles
taHit amrik	at your disposal (lit. under your order)
sheysh jaaj	grilled chicken skewers
dagiigah (pl. dagaayig)	minute; minutes

New expressions

SiHteyn: lit., two healths. This is an expression of wishing that the food brings health to the people who eat it; usually said by the one who serves food or drink.

Your guest comments that the food was delicious. You respond:

> **SiHteyn.**

3ala galbak: lit., at or to your heart. This is a polite answer for the previous expression. It is returning the good wish to the speaker.

In response to the above situation, the guest should say:

> **3ala galbak.**

shuu bituʔmu-ru?: lit., what do you order? This is a polite expression inviting people to ask for a service. Notice the possessive pronoun at the end. This can change to other pronouns as you now know.

law samaHt: lit., if you allow; with your permission. This is a polite expression to follow a request.

bi3yuuni: lit., with my eyes. A polite way of saying you will spare no effort to get something done, or to give some service.

> **mumkin tjiibli ma3ak sandwish, law samaHt?**   **bi3yuuni.**
> Can you get me a sandwich, if you don't mind?   Sure.

tikram: lit., you're honored. A polite expression saying that you will do something for someone.

> **shukran 3ala wagtak.**   **tikram, ahlan wa sahlan.**
> Thanks for your time.   Sure, you're welcome.

HaaDir: lit., present. This means "sure" to express that you will give some service or do what you promised.

taHit amrik: lit., under your orders. The meaning is "at your disposal."

sheysh jaaj: *jaajih (pl. jaaj)* means chicken. The first word, **sheysh**, most likely came from Turkish.

3ashar dagaayig: lit., ten minutes. This is saying how much time it will likely take to get something done. You can use a different number (**dagiigteyn:** two minutes; **xams dagaayig:** five minutes). None of these indicates a real commitment to the time specified. It's just a way of saying that something will be done quite fast.

Dialogue 3 (Audio 1.49)

John is calling a pizza restaurant asking for pizza delivery.

JOHN:	aluu, marHaba
PIZZA PERSON:	ahleyn. tfaDDal
JOHN:	biddi iththneyn biitza wasaT.
PIZZA PERSON:	bituʔmur Habiibi. ay biitza biddak?
JOHN:	waHdih maragriita, bass xuDaar. wa iththaanyih, jaaj ma3 fiTir wa filfil w zeytuun.

PIZZA PERSON: Hajim wasaT?
JOHN: aah, law samaHt wasaT.
PIZZA PERSON: bidna nuSS saa3ah.
JOHN: maashi, mish mushkilih.
PIZZA PERSON: hadool ya sidi bi tis3 dananiir.
JOHN: tikram, ya sidi.
PIZZA PERSON: 3inwaanak, law samaHt.
JOHN: shagah xamsih, 3amaarit ilistiqlaal, shaari3
                iljaam3ah.
PIZZA PERSON: 3ala Tuul. nuSS saa3ah bakuun 3indak.
JOHN: shukran, ma3 issalaamih.

JOHN: *Hello, hi.*
PIZZA PERSON: *Hi, what can I do for you?*
JOHN: *I want two medium pizzas.*
PIZZA PERSON: *At your disposal, which pizza do you want?*
JOHN: *One Margherita, just vegetarian. And the other one is*
                chicken with mushroom, peppers and olives.
PIZZA PERSON: *Medium size?*
JOHN: *Yes, please, medium size.*
PIZZA PERSON: *We will need half an hour.*
JOHN: *OK, no problem.*
PIZZA PERSON: *These, sir, will be JD9.*
JOHN: *Certainly, sir.*
PIZZA PERSON: *Your address, if you please.*
JOHN: *Apartment 5, Istiqlal Building, University St.*
PIZZA PERSON: *Sure. Half an hour and I will be there.*
JOHN: *Thank you, bye!*

Vocabulary

wasaT	medium
biitza	pizza
maragriita	Margherita, vegetarian pizza
bass	only
xuDaar (x+D+r)	vegetables

fiTir; fuTur; mashruum	mushroom
zeytuun	olives
Hajim	size
nuSS	half
mushkilih (pl. mashaakil)	problem
hadool	these
3inwaan+ak	your address
shagah (pl. shugag)	apartment
3amaarah; 3amaarit (pl. 3amaaraat)	building
shaari3 (pl. shawaari3)	street
3ala Tuul	sure, certainly
b+akuun (k+aa+n)	to be

New expressions

bitu?mur Habiibi (fem. bitu?muri Habiibti): lit., you order, darling. This is a polite way of expressing consent to do something or to provide a service. It is commonly used by waiters, mechanics and service providers who expect some kind of tip for their services. It is used within the same gender, i.e., it is not common for a male waiter to say it to female customers. It does not imply any special relationship. The closest in English is the use of "honey" by some American retail store cashiers.

biitza: This is a borrowed word. Keep in mind that native speakers of Arabic will mostly switch the English /p/ to a /b/. This is due to the fact that Arabic consonant inventory does not have this phoneme.

ya sidi (fem. ya sitti): lit., oh, sir; oh, madam. This is a filler showing respect.

3ala Tuul: lit., on or for long. This is used to indicate consent to do something or provide some service.

Exercise 1

Classify the following vocabulary items in groups.

SiHteyn	fuul	bitu?mur	bi3yuuni	mashaawi
salaTah	3ala galbak	bibsi	muqabilaat	mtabbal
gahwah	mHammarah	kibbih	laban	shay
mxlallal	taHit amrik	sheysh jaaj	HummuS	3aSiir (juice)
mayyih	xuDaar	fiTir	zeytuun	3ala Tuul

main dishes	appetizers	drinks	polite service words	polite responses

Exercise 2

Arrange the following statements such that the order of events is logical.

1 kam bikuun liHsaab?
2 tikram.
3 3ala Tuul, ay shi thaani?
4 marHaba.
5 HaaDir.
6 ahlan shabaab, tfaDDalu.
7 liHsaab bikuun thaman dananiir w nuSS.
8 law samaHt, bidna HummuS, fuul, falaafil, mtabbal w
   mHammarah.
9 aah, shay law samaHt.
10 ahlan biik. bidnaa nitghadda, shuu fiih 3indkum ilyoom.
11 haay ilminyu. shuuf shuu btu?mur.

Numbers – extension

In Unit three, we learnt numbers 1–10. See Table 5.1 for numbers 11
and above.

Table 5.1 Numbers 11 and above (**Audio 2.1; Bonus audio 13**)

Number	LA	
11	١١	iHda3ish; ihda3ish; ida3ish
12	١٢	iththna3ish; ittna3ish
13	١٣	thalathTa3ish; thalTTa3ish; talatta3ish
14	١٤	arba3Ta3ish
18	١٨	thamanTa3ish; tamanTa3ish
19	١٩	tisa3Ta3ish
20	٢٠	3ishriin
21	٢١	waaHad w 3ishriin
22	٢٢	thnein w 3ishriin
23	٢٣	thalaath w 3ishriin; talaat w 3ishriin
29	٢٩	tis3ah w 3ishriin
30	٣٠	thalaathiin; talatiin
31	٣١	waaHad w thalaathiin
32	٣٢	thnein w thalaathiin
40	٤٠	arb3iin
90	٩٠	tis3iin
100	١٠٠	miiyih
101	١٠١	miiyih w waaHad
102	١٠٢	miiyih w thnein
103	١٠٣	miiyih w thalaath
110	١١٠	miiyih w 3asharah
111	١١١	miiyih w iHda3ish
200	٢٠٠	miiteyn
300	٣٠٠	thalaath miiyih; talaat miiyih
450	٤٥٠	arba3 miiyih w xamsiin
900	٩٠٠	tisi3 miiyih
1000	١٠٠٠	alf
1990	١٩٩٠	alf w tisi3 miiyih w tis3iin
1876	١٨٧٦	alf w thaman miiyih w sittih w sab3iin
2000	٢٠٠٠	alfeyn
3000	٣٠٠٠	thalaath aalaaf; talaat aalaaf
9000	٩٠٠٠	tisi3 aalaaf
10,000	١٠٠٠٠	3ashar aalaaf
685,431	٦٨٥٤٣١	sitt miiyih w xamsih w thamaniin alf w arba3 miiyih w waaHad w thalaathiin
1,000,000	١٠٠٠٠٠٠	malyoon
2,986,352	٢٩٨٦٣٥٢	thnein malyoon w tisi3 miiyih w sittih w thamaaniin alf w thalaat h miiyih w thnein w xamsiin

The reader should be able to find out a systematic pattern. Wherever the number has 1 or 2 in it, it is better to memorize it. There is a pattern of course but it is worth just memorizing these numbers: 1, 2, 11, 12, 21, 22, 31, 32, etc. Numbers 3 to 9 are very systematic. See Table 5.2.

Table 5.2 Number suffixes

١ – ١٠	١٣ – ١٩	٢٣ – ٢٩	٣٠٠ – ٩٠٠	٣٠٠٠ – ٩٠٠٠	١٠٠٠٠٠٠
memorize	/-Ta3ish/	/-iin/	/-miiyih/	/-aalaaf/	/-malyoon/

Countable nouns

Consider the following examples:

ktaab waaHid	one book
ktaabeyn	two books
thalaath kutub	three books
arba3 kutub	four books
tisi3 kutuub	nine books
iHda3ishar ktaab	eleven books
iththna3ishar ktaab	twelve books
thalathTa3shar ktaab	thirteen books
3ishriin ktaab	twenty books
miit ktaab	one hundred books
alf ktaab	one thousand books
malyoon ktaab	one million books

Notice the addition of /-**ar**/ in the teen category of numbers. It comes from the suffix for ten, /**3ashr**/. As you can see, countable nouns are in singular form with one, followed by the suffix /-**eyn**/ for two and then come in the plural form from 3 to 10, and in the singular form after that.

Exercise 3

Write the following numbers in Arabic transliteration.

1 ٣٤
2 ٥٥
3 ٧٠
4 ١٠٤
5 ١٦٨
6 ٢٨٤٩
7 ٤٠١٢
8 ٨٦٤٣
9 ٢٨٧٣٥٩١
10 ٧٤٣٢٩٠٧

Exercise 4

Translate the following into Arabic. Feel free to use transliteration.

1 Five lectures
2 Two classes
3 Ten days
4 Fifteen offices
5 Twenty-four hours
6 Eighty-eight apartments
7 Three hundred and fifty-five buildings
8 A million dollars
9 Six thousand engineers
10 Five hundred universities

Jordanian currency

Below are the different types of bills used in Jordan. (JD 1 = $1.4; JD 1 = €1.09). One dinar is made up of 100 piasters (piaster = girsh).

xamsiin diinaar	3ishriin diinaar
3ashar danaaniir	xams danaaniir
diinaar waaHad	nuSS diinaar (50 girsh)
rubu3 diinar (25 girsh)	3ashar gruush
xams gruush	girsh waaHad

Exercise 5

If you paid JD5 for each of the following items, how much should you get back?

1 A cup of coffee for 0.70 and a sandwich for 0.80.
2 Took a short taxi ride. The meter displayed 2.45.
3 Bought dinner for your friend at 3.25.
4 The bus fare is 0.72 and you paid JD1.

Tell the time (Audio 2.2)

Since we have learned numbers, we should be able to tell the time. Consider the following:

1:00	waHdih
1:15	waHdih w rubu3
1:20	waHdih w thilith
1:30	waHdih w nuSS
1:45	thinteyn illa rubu3
1:40	thinteyn illa thilith
1:50	thinteyn illa 3ashrah
1:05	waHdih w xams dagaayig
1:55	thinteyn illa xamsih
1:01	waHdih w dagiigah
1:58	thinteyn illa dagiigteyn
1:10	waHdih w 3ashrah

Notice that 20 minutes before the next hour, people shift to using the next hour minus /illa/ the remaining minutes. Also notice the units for 15 minutes, 20, 30.

Exercise 6

Tell the time:

1 4:00	5 12:35
2 7:17	6 1:45
3 9:20	7 6:54
4 10:30	8 8:50

Identifying the letters (م، ن، هـ، و، لا، ي)

Exercise 7

Write each of the following letters three times:

م   و
ن   لا
ه   ي

Exercise 8 (Bonus audio 14)

Join the following letters to make up the words. Add the short vowels where appropriate (where they appear on the letters in isolation). Refer to the transliteration key if you need help. Again, make sure you start from right to left. Now that you have learnt all the letters of the alphabet, you should attempt to write all words in Arabic. Practise reading the words aloud.

1 هُـ م (they)
2 ا ل ل ي ل (the night)
3 أ هـ لا (welcome)
4 مَ ش ا و ي (grilled meat)
5 كَ ب ا ب (kebabs)
6 سَ لَ ط ة (salad)
7 مَ ط عَ م (restaurant)
8 ا لأ ر دُ ن (Jordan)
9 كِ ت ا بَ ة (writing)
10 خُ ض رَ و ا ت (vegetables)

Exercise 9

Identify the letters (ي، لا، و، هـ، ن، م) in the following paragraph. There is no need to worry about the letters you do not know at this time.

م	ن	هـ	و	لا	ي

العراق دولة تقع في شمال غرب العالم العربي. يبلغ عدد سكان العراق حوالي
ستة و ثلاثين مليون نسمة. يحدّه من الشمال تركيا، و من الغرب إيران، من

الجنوب الكويت و السعودية ومن الشرق سوريا و الأردن. تعتبر دولة العراق
واحدة من أقدم الحضارات في العالم. فقد قامت حضارة ما بين بلاد الرافدين قبل
أكثر من ثمانية آلاف سنة، و في العراق تم اختراع الكتابة المسمارية و كان
السومريون من أول الشعوب التي حكمت هذه البلاد. و كانت العراق أيضاً مهداً
للحضارة الاكادية، و الآشورية و البابلية. و بعد ظهور الإسلام انتقلت عاصمة
الدولة الإسلامية اليها في زمن الدولة العباسية. من أهم مدنها بغداد، الموصل،
كربلاء، و البصرة في الجنوب.

Exercise 10 (Bonus audio 15)

If you have the audio, listen to the words, repeat and write them down.

Unit Six

في بيتنا

fii beytna

At our home

In this unit, you will learn about:

- Dining at a family home
- The iDaafah construct
- Months

Dining at a family home

If you get invited to someone's home for lunch or dinner, and most likely you will, you will face a totally different experience compared to dining in a restaurant. If you are invited, you are a guest and guests in the Arab world enjoy lavish service. It is a unique and culturally rich experience that you should not miss. But here are some guidelines.

- If you are invited, decline at first politely, saying that you would love to go but you do not want to burden your hosts. This is generally how it goes: you are invited, then you decline politely, then the host insists and then you accept graciously.
- Once you accept the invitation, and if you know that food will be served, tell the host of any dietary restrictions you might have. If you are vegetarian, you need to specify that you do not eat meat. The host will not feel comfortable if he/she prepares a lot of food and you end up not eating.
- On the day of your visit, dress well – comfortably but decently. You will be going into someone's home and therefore you want to blend in well. Shorts and tank-tops are not advised.
- It is very polite to buy a very simple gift for the family. If the family has a child, for example, bring the equivalent of a $5 toy, etc. If you're going with a group of other visitors, maybe you could all contribute to buying a small gift for your hosts. The value of the gift is not important. The gesture breaks cultural barriers.
- Once you arrive, proceed as directed. Take off your shoes outside the house or outside the guest room, unless instructed otherwise. Sit wherever the host asks you to.
- Some hosts will begin by serving you some Arabian coffee. This type of coffee is strong but usually has some cardamom added to it. You will be offered a small cup with 2–3 sips. You should drink the coffee and return the cup to the host. The host will pour more coffee for you. If you do not want to be served more coffee, you should shake the cup slightly. This is a sign that you do not want any more coffee. This tradition is originally Bedouin but it has permeated in different LA communities.
- Once food is served, you should ask to wash your hands, if you have not washed them earlier. Now there are two sets of etiquettes depending on whether food will be shared from one big plate or if everyone has their own individual plate.

Shared plate:

1 Having washed your hands, wait to be invited to take some food.
2 Once invited, eat using your right hand. In Arab and Muslim culture, the left hand is used to clean oneself in the bathroom. It can therefore be offensive to people to use your left hand for food from a shared plate. If you have to, or if you're left-handed, then ask for a spoon or a fork.
3 Some foods are eaten by hand, not using a spoon or a fork. If you cannot do this or are not comfortable with it, ask for a fork or a spoon.
4 Always eat from the place on the plate closest to you, right in front of you. Do not reach out for food in front of other people.
5 Making loud chewing sounds is frowned upon and dripping food should be avoided.
6 Engage in some light discussions: express how delicious the food is, express thanks to your host, talk about your own food culture, etc.
7 If you need anything else: more bread, water, etc., feel free to ask for it.
8 Do not eat too fast or too slowly.
9 The host will keep asking you to eat more. Once you are full, resist politely saying that the food was really delicious but that you are full and cannot take any more.
10 The host will direct you to a place where you will wash your hands and then come back.
11 In some places, you will come back to the same guest room where food was served. If food was served in a dining room, you will go back to the guest room. Once everyone is done, they will join you.
12 Some people serve food at a dining table. Others serve food on the floor. Either way, you are expected to join and mix with everyone.

Individual plate:
   All of what is mentioned above is expected. There are two major differences, however:

1 Since it is your own plate, you have more freedom of eating the way you want. You do not really have to worry much about reaching in front of someone else.

2 You are expected not to waste a lot of food. You put on your plate as much as you think you will eat. You can go for a second and a third helping but you want to make sure that you will finish your food. In some local cultures, you are not supposed to finish everything on your plate. You can leave two or three spoonfuls. The idea is that the food was so abundant and that your host was so generous but you could not finish it all. This is a fine line: you do not leave so much food that it gets wasted and you do not clean off all of your plate so that your host thinks the food served to you was not enough.

Finally, there will usually be a great deal of tolerance on the part of your host. Most people understand that you come from a different culture and therefore, they are a lot more tolerant. But generally, food culture in LA, and in most places in the Arab world, is rich with dos and don'ts.

Dialogue 1 (Audio 2.3–2.4)

Thomas is invited to Khalid's family for dinner.

XAALID: ahlan toomas, tfaDDal, tfaDDal.
TOOMAS: shukran, shukran. ahlan biik.
Arabian coffee is served.
XAALID: tfaDDal *(handing the coffee cup)*
TOOMAS: shukran, yislamu.
XAALID: ilyoom issitt ilwaaldih 3aamlih mansaf.
TOOMAS: allaah ybaarik fiiha. ghallabtu Haalkum.
XAALID: ?abadan, maa fiih ghalabih.
XAALID: yallah itfaDDal *(bringing in the food plate)*
TOOMAS: maa shaa allaah!
XAALID: yallah bism illaah.
TOOMAS: il?akil bijannin.
XAALID: SiHteyn.
TOOMAS: 3ala galbak.

TOOMAS: alHamdu lillaah! *(after eating enough).*
XAALID: ziid ya toomas, kul kamaan.
TOOMAS: wallah shbi3it. ilHamdu lillaah.
XAALID: ?akiid? SiHteyn.
TOOMAS: sufrah daaymih.

KHALID: *Welcome Thomas, come in, come in!*
THOMAS: *Thanks, thanks, welcome to you.*
Arabian coffee is served.
KHALID: *There you go* (handing him a coffee cup).
THOMAS: *Thanks. Hope they (your hands) are well.*
KHALID: *Today, my mother is making mansaf.*
THOMAS: *May God bless her. You have gone to a lot of trouble/*
          inconvenienced yourselves.
KHALID: *Not at all, there is no trouble.*
KHALID: *OK, there you go* (bringing in the food plate).
THOMAS: *Wow!*
KHALID: *OK, let's eat (in the name of God).*
THOMAS: *The food is great/makes one crazy.*
KHALID: *With health.*
THOMAS: *Health be to your heart.*
THOMAS: *Praise be to God!* (After eating enough)
KHALID: *More, Thomas, eat more.*
THOMAS: *By God I am full. Praise be to Allah.*
KHALID: *Sure? With much health.*
THOMAS: *May this dining be always present!*

Vocabulary

yislamu	may (your hands) be well
mansaf	a plate of rice, lamb or chicken and yogurt soup
ybaarik fi (b+r+k)	to bless someone or something
ghallabtu (gh+l+l+b)	to go to the trouble of; inconvenience someone
Haalkum	yourselves
?abadan	not at all; never
ghalabih (n.)	inconvenience

bism illaah	in the name of God
il+?akil (a+k+l)	food
bi+jannin (j+n+n)	to make crazy (crazy good)
al+Hamdu (H+m+d)	to praise
ziid (z+y+d)	to add or do something more
kul (a+k+l)	eat (v. imperative)
wallah	I swear by God
shbi3it (sh+b+3)	to feel full (of food)
sufrah	dining; the act of dining
daaymih (d+w+m)	continuous; always present

New expressions

yislamu: lit., may they (your hands) be well. This is a polite expression of gratitude when someone has done something good. So, if someone prepared some food for you, a mechanic fixed your car, a waiter served you, etc., you could use this expression.

ybaarik fiik: lit., may (God) bless you; used to express good wishes for someone.

ghallabtu Haalkum: lit., you have inconvenienced yourselves. This expression is used by the one who received some good service. It says that you appreciate that some people took the trouble of doing something.

?abadan: lit., not at all; never. This is a response to the previous expression.

maa fiih ghalabih: lit., there's no problem; no inconvenience. This serves the same function as above.

bism illaah: lit., in the name of God. This expression is heavily used before starting to do something. Most of the time, it's used before starting to eat or drink – that you do it in the name of God. Food and drink are consumed in the hope that they will bring better health. If one starts on a project, using this expression is thought to invoke God so that it succeeds. Some people use this term extensively: before going into someone's house, when starting their cars, before dressing, etc. If in the presence of food, this expression can be used by the host as an invitation for people to start eating.

bi+jannin: lit., it makes one crazy (in a good sense). Used as a compliment. You can use this expression to compliment delicious food, a nice car, a celebrity, a child, a nice office, a nice view, etc.

haadha il beyt bijannin, ya salaam maa aHlaah!
This home makes (me) crazy. How beautiful it is!

ziid: lit., do more. This is an invitation to eat or drink more. It is an imperative verb form but it's very polite.
kul kamaan: lit., eat more. This is an invitation by hosts for guests to eat more food. Eating more food is a sign of appreciation for the host. It makes them feel good that their food was enjoyed.
sufrah daaymih: lit., continuing dining (table). This expression is used by the guest once he/she is full and can take no more food. It's a good wish that the bounty be always available for the host.

Exercise 1

Respond to each of the following statements appropriately:

1 ahlan wa sahlan.
2 tfaDDal *(offering you a cup of tea)*.
3 kul kamaan, ziid.
4 in shaa allaah il?akil kwaayis?
5 SiHteyn.

Exercise 2

Use each of the following words in a short sentence. Write answers in Arabic script. Wherever a root is provided feel free to use different derivations.

1 b+r+k fi
2 ?abadan
3 a+k+l
4 kamaan
5 sh+b+3

Dialogue 2 (Audio 2.5–2.6)

Sara is invited to Salma's house for dinner. They're discussing Sara's food preferences on the phone before Sara's arrival.

SALMA: marHaba saara, kiifik?

SAARA: ahlan salma. mniiHah. inti kiifik?

SALMA: mniiHah. kunt biddi ?sa?lik shuu bitHibi bukrah 3al 3asha??

SAARA: shukran Habiibti salma, ghallabti Haalik.

SALMA: maa fiih ghalabih ?abadan.

SAARA: ana bSaraaHah nabaatiyyih, maa baakul laHmih aw jaaj.

SALMA: maashi, raayiH yikuun fiih faaSuulyia ma3 laHmih, w xuDaar mshakkalih ma3 jaaj.

SAARA: bass ana nabaatiyyih, maa baakul laHmih wa la jaaj.

SALMA: Tayyib, mumkin samak ma3 xudaar?

SAARA: kamaan ma baHibb issamak. mumkin aakul HummuS w falaafil.

SALMA: HummuS w falaafil? iHna mish maT3am.

SAARA: maashi, mumkin aakul 3adas w bandoorah?

SALMA: bass heyk? 3adas w bandoorah?

SAARA: mmm *(thinking, not knowing what to say)*

SALMA: maashi, maashi saara, ba3deyn baHki ma3ik, yallah bay.

SAARA: maashi, ma3 issalaamih.

SALMA: *Hello Sara, how are you?*

SARA: *Hello Salma, (I'm) good, how are you?*

SALMA: *Good. I was going to ask what you would like (to eat) tomorrow for dinner.*

SARA: *Thanks, darling. You have inconvenienced yourself.*

SALMA: *Not at all.*

SARA: *Honestly, I'm vegetarian; I do not eat meat or chicken.*

SALMA: *OK. There will be white beans with meat and vegetables with chicken.*

SARA: *But I'm vegetarian. I do not eat meat or chicken.*

SALMA: *OK. (How about) fish and vegetables?*

SARA: *Again, I do not like fish. I can eat hummus and falafel.*

SALMA: *Hummus and falafel? We are not a restaurant.*
SARA: *OK, I can eat some lentils and tomatoes?*
SALMA: *Just that, lentils and tomatoes?*
SARA: *Mmm* (thinking, not knowing what to say).
SALMA: *OK, OK Sara, I will call you later. Bye.*
SARA: *OK, Bye.*

Vocabulary

mniiHah	good, well
ʔasaʔlik (s+ʔ+l)	I ask you
bitHibbi (H+b+b)	you (fem.) like
3ashaʔ	dinner
Habiibti	my darling
b+SaraaHah	frankly
nabaatiyyih (nabaati+fem.)	vegetarian
baakul (ʔ+k+l)	to eat
laHmih	meat (red meat)
jaaj	chicken (white meat)
maashi	OK, fine, sure
raayiH (r+w+H)	to go
faaSuulyia	(Italian) white beans
xuDaar	vegetables
mshakkalih (mshakkal+fem.)	mixed
samak	fish
kamaan	again, besides, in addition to
3adas	lentils
bandoorah	tomatoes
bass heyk	just that
ba3deyn	later

New expressions

mniiH/mniiHa: originally **maliiH, maliiHah** meaning good-looking or beautiful.

    kunt biddi: I was going to.

    kaanat bidha tnaam issaa3ah 3ashrah, bass gultilha bakkiir.
She was going to sleep at 10:00 but I told her it was early.

Habiibti: my darling. This is an endearment term; equivalent to English "honey." It can be used to express a special love relationship, or to simply express endearment. The latter usage is largely restricted to exchanges within the same gender.

Exercise 3

Fill in the blanks with the correct word from the lists of vocabulary in this unit. A list of possible words is provided, but feel free to provide different answers.

ilHamdu	3aamliin	ba3deyn
mumkin	bitHibi	ybaarik

1 bukrah maama w baaba _____ jaaj ma3 xuDaar 3ala il3asha?.
2 allaah _____ fiihum.
3 ana shbi3it, _____ lillaah.
4 shuu _____ ilyoom 3al 3asha??
5 ma baHibb ilmansaf _____ maa aakul ilyoom?

Exercise 4

Match the expressions and their appropriate answers.

1 ghallabtu Haalkum   A itfaDDali
2 il?akil bijannin   B allaah ydiimak
3 yislamu   C ziid, kul kamaan
4 mumkin ?asa?lik su?aal?   E SiHteyn
5 shbi3it   D maa fiih ghalabih
6 sufrah daaymih   F allaah ysallmik

The iDaafah construct

iDaafah, literally addition, is a prevalent construct in Arabic through which one indefinite noun is added to a definite noun, which results in a new definite compound noun. Let's consider the following examples:

1 **beyt xaalid**   Khalid's house
2 **rijl ilkursi**   the chair leg
3 **SaHin HummuS**   hummus dish
4 **yoom ilaHad**   Sunday
5 **madiinat nyuu yoork**   New York city

Each of the above examples is made of two nouns: the first noun is indefinite and the second noun is definite. Adding the first noun to the second one makes the new compound noun definite. In addition to definition by the definite article (**galam**; **ilgalam** – pen; the pen); and definition by possessive pronoun (**galam**; **gamali** – pen; my pen), Arabic utilizes iDaafah to express definiteness. As you can see, sometimes iDaafah expresses possessiveness (as in examples 1 and 2, above) and at other times, it uses the second noun to specify or define the first one. This structure is very prevalent in both MSA as well as LA. The iDaafah construct is not to be confused with the noun-adjective structure. In an iDaafah construct, the two nouns are different in terms of their definiteness: the first is indefinite, the second is usually definite. The iDaafah construct therefore serves the goal of changing from indefinite to definite. A noun-adjective structure, however, can be distinguished by the fact that the two units (the noun and the adjective) are identical in their definiteness. If the first noun in an iDaafah construct ends in the feminine marker (/-ah/, or /-ih/), it changes to (/-at/, /-it/) in pronunciation. If it is a noun-adjective string, the pronunciation remains (/-ah/, /-ih/). This is a phonetic, not a spelling rule. See the examples below:

1 **sayyaarah jadiidih**   a new car
2 **sayyaarit xaalid**   Khalid's car
3 **madiinah Sagheirah**   a small town/city
4 **madiinat dimashq**   the city of Damascus
5 **dawlah kabiirah**   a big country
6 **dawlat albaHreyn**   the country of Bahrain

Exercise 5

Read the following text and find examples of the iDaafah construct and examples of subject-adjective structures. Fill in the table below appropriately.

العراق دولة تقع في شمال غرب العالم العربي. يبلغ عدد سكان العراق حوالي ستة و ثلاثين مليون نسمة. يحدّه من الشمال تركيا، و من الغرب إيران، من الجنوب الكويت و السعودية ومن الشرق سوريا و الأردن. تعتبر دولة العراق واحدة من أقدم الحضارات في العالم. فقد قامت حضارة ما بين بلاد الرافدين قبل أكثر من ثمانية آلاف سنة، و في العراق تم اختراع الكتابة المسمارية و كان السومريون من أول الشعوب التي حكمت هذه البلاد. و كانت العراق أيضاً مهداً للحضارة الاكادية، و الآشورية و البابلية. و بعد ظهور الإسلام انتقلت عاصمة الدولة الإسلامية اليها في زمن الدولة العباسية. من أهم مدنها بغداد، الموصل، كربلاء، و البصرة في الجنوب.

noun-adjective phrase	iDaafah

Exercise 6

Match each of the following phrases to their Arabic translations. Then decide whether each phrase is an iDaafah construct.

Arabic	English	Answers	iDaafah (Y/N)
1 بيت أخي	a delicious food	1 _____	_____
2 أكل طيب	b my brother's home	2 _____	_____
3 بيت جديد	c pizza restaurant	3 _____	_____
4 مطعم البيتزا	d the door of the house	4 _____	_____
5 باب البيت	e a new house	5 _____	_____

Months of the year

In LA, the year follows the Gregorian calendar. The same applies to all Arab countries except Saudi Arabia and some other Gulf countries.

In written Arabic, the Arabic names of the months of the year are commonly used. In spoken Levantine Arabic, it's customary to use the month number to refer to dates rather than the month name. See Dialogue 3. When giving a date, people usually give the day, followed by the month and then the year. Table 6.1 below presents months of the year.

Table 6.1 Months of the year **(Audio 2.7)**

No.	MSA		LA			English
1	كانون الثاني	shahr waaHad	شهر واحد	كانون الثاني	kaanuun iththaani	January
2	شباط	shahr ithnein	شهر اثنين	شباط	shbaaT	February
3	آذار	shahr thalaathih	شهر ثلاث	آذار	aadhaar	March
4	نيسان	shahr arba3ah	شهر اربعة	نيسان	neysaan	April
5	أيار	shahr xamsih	شهر خمسة	أيار	ayyaar	May
6	حزيران	shahr sittih	شهر ستة	حزيران	Huzayraan	June
7	تموز	shahr sab3ah	شهرسبعة	تموز	tammuuz	July
8	آب	shahr thamaanyih	شهر ثمانية	آب	aab	August
9	أيلول	shahr tis3ah	شهر تسعة	أيلول	ayluul	September
10	تشرين الأول	shahr 3asharah	شهر عشرة	تشرين الأول	tishriin il?awwal	October
11	تشرين الثاني	shahr ihda3ish	شهر اهدعش	تشرين الثاني	tishriin iththaani	November
12	كانون الاول	shahr ithna3ish	شهر اثنعش	كانون الاول	kaanuun il?awwal	December

Dialogue 3 (Audio 2.8–2.9)

Khalid and Asma work at a language center. They are planning the calendar of events until the end of the semester.

XAALID: marHaba asma, keyfik?

ASMA: ahlan xaalid, ana tamaam. laazim niHki 3an xuTTit innashaaTaat.

XAALID: ?akiid. ilbarnaamij bibda? bishahr sittih.

ASMA: shuu fiih bishahr sittih w sab3ah?

XAALID: shahr sittih ziyaarat 3ajloon w jarash, w shahr sab3ah ramadan, ma fiih shi.

ASMA: tamaam. shahr thamanyih riHlih li irbid wa um qays.

XAALID: mumtaaz. shahr tis3ah 3iid ilaDHa.

ASMA: Tayyib. shahr 3asharah ilbatra.
XAALID: ?akiid. shuu ra?yak shahr ihda3ish waadi ram w il3agabih?
ASMA: fikrah mumtaazih. wa shahr iththna3ish imtiHaanaat.

KHALID: *Hello Asma, how are you?*
ASMA: *Hello Khalid, I'm good. We need to talk about the plan for activities.*
KHALID: *Sure. The program starts in the month of June (in the 6th month).*
ASMA: *What is there in June and July?*
KHALID: *(In) June a visit to Ajloun and Jarash, and (in) July (there will be) Ramadan. There is nothing.*
ASMA: *Perfect. (In) August (there will be) a trip to Irbid and Um Qais (Jadara).*
KHALID: *Excellent. (In) September (there will be) Eid Al-Adha.*
ASMA: *Fine. Petra is October.*
KHALID: *Sure. What do you think about (visiting) Wadi Rum and Aqaba in November?*
ASMA: *Excellent idea. And December is (the month of) exams.*

Vocabulary

niHki 3an (H+k+y 3an)	to talk about
xuTat (pl. xuTatT)	plan
nashaaTaat (sing. nashaaT)	activities
barnaamij (pl. baraamij)	program
bibda? (b+d+?)	to start
ziyaarat (sing. ziyaarah)	visits
riHlih (pl. riHlaat)	trip
3iid	festival
ilaDHa	sacrifice
3iid ilaDHa	Eid Al-Adha (Festival of Sacrifice)
Tayyib	OK, sure
ray (pl. aaraa?)	opinion
fikrah (pl. afkaar)	idea
imtiHaanaat (sing. imtiHaan)	test, exam

Exercise 7

Answer each of the following questions using day-month-year format.

1 When do you celebrate Independence Day?
2 When did you first travel outside of your country?
3 When were you born?
4 When is your 40th birthday?
5 When is your parents' anniversary?

Exercise 8

In Dialogue 3, both Khalid and Asma use expressions that signal their agreement with a statement. Write down all the words and expressions that they use to serve this function.

Exercise 9

The following statements are taken from Dialogues 1–3 in this unit. Match the English to the Arabic origin.

	English			عربي	
1	ahlan toomas, tfaDDal, tfaDDal	a	ممكن آكل عدس و بندورة؟	1 ___
2	shukran, shukran. ahlan biik	b	شكراً، شكراً، أهلاً بيك	2 ___
3	maa shaa allaah	c	ماشي، مع السلامة	3 ___
4	marHaba saara, w inti kiifik?	d	مرحبا سارة، و انتي كيفك؟	4 ___
5	HummuS w falaafil	e	فكرة ممتازة	5 ___
6	mumkin aakul 3adas w bandoorah?	f	أهلاً توماس، تفضّل، تفضّل	6 ___
7	maashi, ma3 issalaamih	g	ما شاء الله	7 ___
8	mumtaaz. shahr tis3ah 3iid ilaDHa	h	ممتاز، شهر تسعة عيد الأضحى	8 ___
9	Tayyib. shahr 3asharah ilbatra	i	حمص و فلافل	9 ___
10	fikrah mumtaazih	j	طيب، شهر عشرة البترا	10 ___

Exercise 10

Conjugate the verb (**s+ʔ+l**: to ask).

Pronoun	Translation	s+ʔ+l
1 **ana**	I	_____
2 **iHna**	we	_____
3 **intah**	you (sing. masc.)	_____
4 **inti**	you (sing. fem.)	_____
5 **intum**	you (pl. masc.)	_____
6 **intin**	you (pl. fem.)	_____
7 **huwwa**	he; it (masc.)	_____
8 **hiyya**	he; it (fem.)	_____
9 **humma**	they (pl. masc.)	_____
10 **hinnih**	they (pl. fem.)	_____

Exercise 11

Write sentences using the verb in Exercise 10 above with five different pronouns. Keep in mind that this verb needs an object.

Example: ana saʔalt ummi 3an amriika.
xaali saʔalni 3an iljaam3ah.

Exercise 12 (Bonus audio 20)

If you have the audio, listen to the words and phrases, repeat and write them down.

Unit Seven

وين نروح؟
weyn nruuH?

Where shall we go?

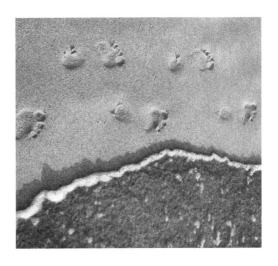

In this unit, you will learn about:

- Cultural activities in leisure time
- Giving directions
- Colors
- How much/how many
- **3ind, ma3, fii**
- The relative pronoun **illi**
- The past tense

Where to go?

In Arab culture, it is customary for people to go out to socialize together. This mostly happens after work, usually in the evening or at night. The most popular hangouts are cafés. While these types of activities are mostly gender-biased – more men than women go out – there is an increasing number of young women going out to cafés and other recreational places.

Dialogue 1 (Audio 2.10–2.11)

Thomas and Mary are at a café in downtown Amman.

GARSOON:	ahlan wa sahlan, itfaDDalu.
MEYRI:	ahlan beik. biddi kaasit shay, law samaHt.
GARSOON:	HaaDir, w inta ya ustaadh?
TOOMAS:	mumkin funjaan gahwah wa ʔargiilih?
GARSOON:	keyf bitHibbi issukkar ya aaniseh?
MEYRI:	wasaT, allaah yxaliik. w ma3 na3na3.
GARSOON:	HaaDir. w keyf gahwtak ya ustaadh?
TOOMAS:	saada.
GARSOON:	wa ilʔargiilih?
TOOMAS:	shuu 3indkum ʔaragiil? shu innakhaat?
GARSOON:	fiih tuffaaHteyn, faraawlih, na3na3, leymuun, shummaam, w fiih na3na3 3ala leymuun.
TOOMAS:	mumkin tuffaaHteyn. bass zabbiTT-ha allaah yxaliik.
GARSOON:	3ala raasi. w inti ya aaniseh, shuu ʔargiiltik?
MEYRI:	ana maa badaxxiin, shukran.
GARSOON:	aHsanlik.

WAITER:	*Welcome, what can I do for you?*
MARY:	*Welcome to you. I'd like a cup of tea, please.*
WAITER:	*Sure, and you, sir?*
THOMAS:	*May I get a cup of coffee and a hookah?*
WAITER:	*How do you like the sugar, madam?*
MARY:	*Medium, please, with mint.*
WAITER:	*Sure and how would you like your coffee, Sir?*

THOMAS:	*Sugar-free.*
WAITER:	*And the hookah?*
THOMAS:	*What hookahs do you have? What flavors are available?*
WAITER:	*There is double apple, strawberry, mint, lemon, melon, and there is mint with lemon.*
THOMAS:	*Double apple, please. But do it well, may Allah keep you.*
WAITER:	*Sure. And you, madam, what hookah would you like?*
MARY:	*I do not smoke, thank you.*
WAITER:	*Good for you.*

Vocabulary

kaasih (pl. kaasaat)	glass
funjaan (p. fanajiin)	cup
ʔargiilih (pl. ʔaraagiil)	hookah
yxaliik (x+l+l+y)	to keep, to leave, to let go
na3na3	mint
saada	sugar-free
nakha (pl. nakhaat)	flavor
tuffaaHah (pl. tuffaaH)	apple
faraawlih	strawberry
leymuun	lemon
shummaam	melons
zabbiTT-ha (z+b+T)	to fix; to do something well
badaxxin (d+x+x+n)	to smoke
aHsan+li	better for

New expressions

keyf bitHibb: how do you like? This is a question that people usually ask before they prepare your coffee or tea in homes or restaurants. In some restaurants, they bring tea or coffee without sugar but provide sugar on the side.

wasaT: medium. This is one answer to the question "how do you like your tea or sugar?"

saada: plain. This is another answer to the question "how do you like your tea or sugar?"

The levels of sweetness usually apply for hot drinks. Here are the most commonly used:

sukkar zyaadih (Hilu)	wasaT/3aadi	saada
sweet/with extra sugar	medium/regular	sugar-free

Some people choose to say "**foog ilwasaT**" or "**taHt ilwasaT**" meaning a little over medium or a little under medium.

shuu 3indkum: what do you have? A question about options for food, drink, etc. Sometimes, this can be a question about current events, similar to saying "what's going on?"

zabbiTT+obj.: lit., fix someone or something: this is a request to do something well. This expression is mostly used at cafés, restaurants or government offices that offer some service. The goal is to encourage the service provider to do it well.

allaah yxaliik: lit., may Allah keep you. This is a very common expression of good wishes to someone. It is used either to express gratitude or to encourage someone to do something (e.g. offer a favor).

3ala raasi: lit., over my head: an expression of respect and promise to do the best. When someone asks you for something, you can respond by saying "**3ala raasi**." This means that you'll be glad to offer your service.

aHsanlik: lit., better for you. It could mean exactly this, and it could be sarcastic, depending on context and tone.

Exercise 1

Rearrange these words in groups where every group contains words of related meanings. Guess meanings of new words first. Use the glossary at the end of the book should you need to.

kaasih	saa3ah	funjaan	na3na3	saada	nakhaha
tuffaaHah	faraawlih	leymuun	shummaam	duxxaan	tamaam
?argiilih	fuul	shay	mashaawi	maT3am	ghada
garSoon	mayyih	sukkar	Hsaab	gahwah	dananiir
salaTah	laban	mxlallal	sheysh jaaj	dagiigah	bidaxxin

Giving directions

Being able to give directions is a very important skill. While one would often use a GPS device in most North American or European countries, you will be compelled to ask people for directions in most Arab countries. Even if you take a taxi, most drivers will know the major roads but they might not know the exact location. In most Arab countries, streets have names and numbers and people use these names and numbers to give directions. But it is also very likely that they will use a major landmark as a point of reference.

 Dialogue 2 **(Audio 2.12)**

 Mary is taking a taxi to her apartment. She is giving directions to the cab driver.

MEYRI:	twaSilni ilbeyt law samaHt.
SAWWAAG:	iTla3i. weyn il3inwaan?
MEYRI:	gariib min jariidit iddustuur.
SAWWAAG:	mashi, 3ala ishshaari3 irraʔiisi?
MEYRI:	la, gharb ishshaari3 irraʔiisi.
SAWWAAG:	ana sawwaag jdiid, ma ba3rif ishshawaari3 mniiH.
MEYRI:	mish mushkilih.
SAWWAAG:	Tayyib, haay binaayit iddustuur, weyn ʔaruuH?
MEYRI:	yamiin Hawaali miit mitir, ba3deyn shmaal.
SAWWAAG:	maashi, w ba3deyn?
MEYRI:	thaani shaari3 3alyamiin, ba3deyn dughri la3ind suber maarkit alwakiil.
SAWWAAG:	aah, 3riftha.
MEYRI:	kamaan Hawaali xamsiin mitir, fiih daxlih 3ashshmaal.
SAWWAAG:	maashi.
MEYRI:	aywah, hoon.
SAWWAAG:	tfaDDali.
MEYRI:	kam ilʔujrah?
SAWWAAG:	diinaar w nuSS.
MEYRI:	tfaDDal.
SAWWAAG:	shukran, ma3 issalaamih.

MARY:	*Can you take me home, please.*
TAXI DRIVER:	*Come in, where is the address?*
MARY:	*Close to Addustur Newspaper.*
TAXI DRIVER:	*Sure, on the main street?*
MARY:	*No, west of the main street.*
TAXI DRIVER:	*I'm a new driver. I do not know the streets well.*
MARY:	*No problem.*
TAXI DRIVER:	*OK. This is the Addustur building. Where shall I go?*
MARY:	*Right for about 100 meters, then left.*
TAXI DRIVER:	*OK, and then?*
MARY:	*Second street to the right, then straight to Supermarket Alwakeel.*
TAXI DRIVER:	*Oh, I know it.*
MARY:	*And after almost fifty meters there is a side street to the left.*
TAXI DRIVER:	*OK.*
MARY:	*Yes, here.*
TAXI DRIVER:	*There you go.*
MARY:	*How much is the fare?*
TAXI DRIVER:	*One and a half dinars.*
MARY:	*Here you go.*
TAXI DRIVER:	*Thanks, goodbye.*

Vocabulary

twaSilni (w+S+S+l)	to give a ride to; to deliver
iTla3i (T+l+3)	to ride up; to become
3inwaan (pl. 3anawiin)	address
jariidih (pl. jaraayid)	newspaper
shaari3 (pl. shawaari3)	street
ra?iisi	main
sawwaag (pl. sawwaagiin)	driver
jdiid or jadiid	new
binaayih (pl. binaayaat)	building
Hawaali	almost

mitir (pl. mtaar)	meter
(duuz) dughri	straight
3rift (3+r+f)	to know
daxlih (pl. daxlaat)	side street
ʔujrah	(taxi) fare

Other words and expressions might be used in giving directions; see Table 7.1.

Table 7.1 Directions **(Audio 2.13)**

Arabic	English	Arabic	English
shamaal	north	hnaak	there
januub	south	ruuH	go
sharg	east	luff/liff	turn
gharb	west	irja3	go back
yamiin	right	intabih	be careful, pay
shmaal/yasaar	left		attention
3ala ilyamiin	to the right	utustraad	highway
3ala ishmaal/	to the left	shaari3 raʔiisi	main street
ilyasaar		daxlih	small street
(duuz) dughri	straight	jisir	bridge
3ala Tuul	straight	mamarr mushaah	pedestrian crossing
ba3iid	far	nafag	tunnel
gariib	close	ʔawwal ishshaari3	first street
ba3d/ba3id	after	ʔaaxir ishshaari3	last street
gabil	before	duwwaar	circle
wara	behind	ishaarah Dawiiyih	traffic light
guddaam	in front of	bsurr3ah	fast
janb/bijanb	to the side of	shawi shawi	slowly
hoon	here	3ala mahlak	slowly

Exercise 2

Describe to your new roommate how to get from your apartment to the nearest restaurant on foot.

Colors

Colors in Arabic are adjectives. Therefore, each color has two different forms: one for describing masculine entities, another for describing feminine entities. But gender agreement is not uniform because of the simple fact that a few colors are very similar to nisba forms. For example, the color "brown" is associated with the color of roasted coffee /**bunn**/, so the color is the nisba form of /**bunn**/; in other words, "of the color of roasted coffee." Another example is "**ramaadi**" from the word /**ramaad**/, which is Arabic for "ashes." Therefore, the feminine form is going to be similar to nisba feminine forms. See Table 7.2.

Table 7.2 Colors **(Audio 2.14; Bonus audio 23)**

Masc.	Fem.		Masc.	Fem.	
abyaD	beiDa	white	burdgaani	burdgaaniiyih	orange
aswad	soda	black	kuHli	kuHliiyih	navy blue
aHmar	Hamra	red	samaawi	samaawiiyih	sky blue
aSfar	Safra	yellow	zahri	zahriiyih	pink
azrag	zarga	blue	banafsaji	banafsajiiyih	purple
axDar	xaDra	green	fiDDi	fiDDiiyih	silver
ramaadi	ramadiiyih	gray	dhahabi	dhahabiiyih	golden
bunni	bunniiyih	brown	beij	beij	beige
faatiH	faatHah	light	ghaamig	ghaamgah	dark

Expressions using colors

galbuh/galbha abyaD: his/her heart is white. Used to describe some-one who does not feel malice or hatred for others. (Opposite meaning: **glabuh/galbha aswad**).

   xaalid galbuh aswad, ma biHibbak ?abadan.
   Khalid's heart is black. He does not like you at all. (Khalid is mean, hateful.)

Tariig xaDra: green route, green road. Wishing someone an easy path, with no obstacles. This is primarily used when someone is about to set out on a trip.

in shaa allaah Tariigak xaDra
I hope your route is green. (Hope you have no obstacles.)

3eyn Hamra: a red eye. Taking a firm stand on something; not willing to yield.

farjiihum il3eyn ilHamra.
Show them the red eye. (Be decisive, be strong, show no weakness.)

Exercise 3

Using the internet, find flags for the following countries and then answer the questions that follow:

Countries: faransa, bariTaanya, maSr, ilurdun, amriika, libnaan, li3raag, issweyd, ilyaabaan.

1 shuu alwan il3alam ilfaransi?
2 shuu alwan il3alam ilyaabaani?
3 shuu alwan il3alam ilurduni?
4 kam loon fi il3alam ilamriiki?
5 kam loon fil il3alam issweydi?
6 shuu il?alwaan illi bittHibha?

Dialogue 3 (Audio 2.15)

Between classes, Ameerah and Ronda chat about clothing during a coffee break.

RUNDA:	kiifik amiirah?
AMIIRAH:	ahlan runda, ana mniiHah. shuu ra?yik nishrab ?ahwih?
RUNDA:	ya reyt. yallah.
AMIIRAH:	runda, ?amiiSik haada Hilu ktiir. w loonuh ktiir shiik.
RUNDA:	shukran. ana baHibb illoon ilaxDar. baHibb kamaan ilaHmar w ilaSafar.
AMIIRAH:	ktiir Hilu 3aleyki. ana shuft mitluh bass maa fiih nafs illoon.
RUNDA:	haada min amriika. mumkin ykuun mitluh bimakkah mool.
AMIIRAH:	bikam ishtareytiih?
RUNDA:	maa ba3rif. maama jaabatuh hadiyyih.
AMIIRAH:	aah! ya3ni maa bit3rafi ?adeish tamanuh?

RUNDA: laa maa ba3rif.

AMIIRAH: Tayyib, ana halla mashghuulih. bashuufik ba3deyn.

RUNDA: bay.

AMIIRAH: bay.

RONDA: *How are you Ameerah?*

AMEERAH: *Hello Ronda, I'm good. Would you like (for us) to have a cup of coffee?*

RONDA: *Yes. Let's do it.*

AMEERAH: *Ronda, your shirt is so beautiful, and its color is so elegant.*

RONDA: *Thanks. I love the green color. I also love red and yellow.*

AMEERAH: *So beautiful on you. I saw one like it but not the same color.*

RONDA: *This is from America. There might be one like it in Mecca Mall.*

AMEERAH: *How much did you buy it for?*

RONDA: *I do not know. My mother brought it as a gift.*

AMEERAH: *Oh! So you do not know how much it is?*

RONDA: *No, I do not know.*

AMEERAH: *OK. Now I'm busy. I'll see you later.*

RONDA: *Bye.*

AMEERAH: *Bye.*

Vocabulary

nishrab (sh+r+b)	to drink
ʔamiiS or gamiiS	shirt
shiik	elegant; good-looking
mitl or mitil	like, similar to
nafs	same as
ishtareytiih (ʔ+sh+t+r+y)	to buy
jaabatuh (j+y+b)	to bring
hadiyyih (pl. hadaaya)	gift
taman or thaman	price
ya3ni (3+n+y)	to mean; it means
mashghuul	busy

New expressions

ya reyt: lit., it's a wish. An expression used when one wants to express that something happens. Sometimes, it is used to express that one would love to do something but you cannot due to some reason.

A friend of yours calls you asking if he could borrow JD100 from you. You say:

miit diinaar? ya reyt. wallah maa ma3i.
A hundred dinars? I wish. I swear I don't have (any money).

Hilu 3aleyki: lit., pretty on you. This expression is used to compliment someone's dress, clothing in general.

Exercise 4

Use each of the following words or expressions in a short sentence. Feel free to derive a different form of the word given.

1 mashghuul
2 thaman
3 hadiyyih
4 nafs
5 ya reyt

Exercise 5

Divide the following words into three grammatical categories: nouns, verbs, or particles or connectors:

Words			Verbs	Nouns	Particles
yxaliik	na3na3	nakaha			
zabbiTTha	badaxxin	twaSilni			
iTla3i	3inwaan	jariidih			
shaari3	sawwaag	binaayih			
Hawaali	3rift	nishrab			
gamiiS	mitil	nafs			
jaabatuh	hadiyyih	Haraarah			
dawa	maa	haay			

Dialogue 4 (Audio 2.16–2.17)

Muna calls the pharmacy asking about some medication.

MUNA:	aluu, Sayydalliiyit ilmanaar?
PHARMACIST:	itfaDDali madaam.
MUNA:	fiih 3indak dawa lil Haraarah?
PHARMACIST:	mawjuud. lamiin iddawa?
MUNA:	la?ibni, 3induh Haraarah, 3umruh santeyn.
PHARMACIST:	salaamtuh. fiih dawa urduni bdiinaar w rubu3. il?ajnabi bthalaath dananiir.
MUNA:	il?ajanbi, law samaHt.
PHARMACIST:	bass si3ruh ghaali.
MUNA:	maa fiih mushkilih. si3ruh fiih.
PHARMACIST:	maashi. itfaDDali w bikuun iddawa jaahiz.
MUNA:	shukran, ma3 issalaamih.

MUNA:	*Hello, Alamanar Pharmacy?*
PHARMACIST:	*Yes, madam.*
MUNA:	*Do you have a medication for fever?*
PHARMACIST:	*It is available, for whom is the medicine?*
MUNA:	*For my son. He has a fever. He's two years old.*
PHARMACIST:	*I wish him well. There is a Jordanian medication for one and a quarter dinar. The foreign (imported) medication is three dinars.*
MUNA:	*The foreign one please.*
PHARMACIST:	*But it is expensive.*
MUNA:	*No problem. It is worth the price.*
PHARMACIST:	*Sure. Come in and it will be ready.*
MUNA:	*Thanks, goodbye.*

Vocabulary

Sayydalliiyih (pl. Sayydalliiyaat)	pharmacy
Haraarah	fever
mawjuud	available
miin	who (lamin: for whom?)
dawa (pl. ?adwiyih)	medication
?ibn (pl. ?abnaa)	son
3umr (pl. a3maar)	age
sanih (pl. sniin or saniin)	year
salaamih	wellness; peace
rubu3 (pl. rbaa3)	quarter
?ajnabi (pl. ajaanib)	foreign; foreigner
si3r (pl. as3aar)	price
jaahiz	ready

New expressions

3induh Haraarah: he has a temperature. This expression is used to say that someone has a fever.

salaamih+pronoun, e.g., salaamtuh, salaamtak. This expression is used to wish someone good health, safe travels or to welcome someone home after returning from a trip.

dawa urduni vs. **dawa ?ajnabi:** Jordanian medication vs. foreign (imported) medication. Jordanians (and most Arabs as well) have a preference for imported goods. Imported goods from China are usually an exception as these are not trusted. This is based on a common belief that Chinese products do not last long or are not very effective, although many people buy them because they are cheap.

si3ruh fiih: it has its price. This expression is used when to refer to some expensive merchandise whose value is worth the price.

Exercise 6

Which is the odd word out?

1 kaasih	funjaan	argiilih	SaHin
2 saadah	wasaT	Hilu	na3na3
3 tuffaaHah	faraawlih	shummaam	leymuun
4 3inwaan	shaari3	daxlih	Hawaali
5 Sayydalliyih	Haraarah	dawa	mithil

How much/how many

Expressions used to ask about quantity do not have much variation in LA. Usually, the question word (equivalent to how much/how many) is followed by a noun phrase. There is no need to use a verb. Table 7.3 shows questions using the equivalent of how much/how many along with possible answers.

Table 7.3 Asking about quantity

	Arabic	English	Arabic	English
1	gaddeish/ Ɂaddeish	how much (is the price of)	bkamm	how much (is the price of)
2	kam	how much/ how many	Ɂachammin[1] (kam -min)	how many

1 This is a local version of the question. Remember that /**k**/ becomes [**ch**] in some rural dialects.

The expressions in 1 are used to ask about the price of something. The expressions in 2 can be used for the same functions but they are more often used to ask about the quantity (not the price) of something.

Exercise 7 (Bonus audio 24)

Answer each of the following questions.

1 kam sanah 3umrak?
2 gaddeish thaman sayyaartak?
3 gaddeish thaman fusTaanik?
4 bikaam ishtareyti ktaab il3arabi?
5 kam marrah zurt ilurdun?

Exercise 8

Ask questions to fit the answers provided.

1 bixamsiin dular.
2 thneyn w 3ishriin sanih.
3 thaman aalaaf dular.
4 bass diinaar w nuSS.
5 arba3 danaaniir.

3ind, ma3, fii

3ind is an adverb of place or time; it specifies where or when something happens. **ma3** can be a preposition that usually means association: something that is associated to someone/something else. It can also be an adverb or place or time. **fii** in LA means there is/are, or better "there exists" (not the same as **fi** in MSA, which is a preposition). These three particles are used to express possessiveness or the fact that something exists somewhere. They can sometimes be interchangeable. Consider the following examples:

1	**3indi muHaaDHarah**	I have a lecture
2	**3ndi/ma3i ijaazih ilyoom**	I have leave today
3	**3indi/ma3i Haraarah**	I have a fever
4	**xaalid bishtaghil 3indak?**	Khalid works for you?
5	**xaalid bishtaghil ma3ak?**	Khalid works with you?
6	**ma3i xamsiin diinaar**	I have fifty dinars
7	**3indi/ma3i sayyaarah jdiidih**	I have a new car
8	**3indi mushkilih kbiirih**	I have a big problem
9	**ma3i/3inid fluwanza ilyoom**	I have flu today
10	**ma3i/3indi waaladeyn w bint**	I have two boys and a girl
11	**fiih mashaakil bissayyaarah**	I have problems with the car
12	**fiih 3indak shay?**	Have you (got some) tea?
13	**maa fiih daa3i txaaf**	There is no reason (for you to) fear
14	**maa ma3i wala girsh**	I do not have any penny (I have not a penny)
15	**maa 3ndi maani3 truuH ma3na**	I have no objection to you going with us
16	**ma3i/3indi thalath saa3aat bass**	I have three hours only

Exercise 9

Translate each of the following sentences into Arabic.

1 I don't have a car.
2 I have a vacation tomorrow.
3 There's a library in my home.
4 Is there a restaurant in this street?
5 Do you have some tea, please?

The relative pronoun *illi*

Relative pronouns are used to link sentences where one noun serves as the subject of two verbs. Consider the following example from English and their translations.

1 I saw the boy *who* was playing football.
   shuft ilwalad *illi* kaan yil3ab faTbool.
2 I have not visited the town *which* you were talking about.
   ana maa zurt ilmadiinih *illi* intah kunt tiHki 3anha.
3 The girl *whose* phone was lost was so sad.
   ilbint *illi* Daa3 talifoonha kaanat Haziinih kthiir.

As you can see, English uses a different relative pronoun depending on the noun to which it refers. Levantine Arabic uses /*illi*/ for all relative pronouns – see the translations. The only rule you need to observe here is that the noun to which the relative pronoun refers must be definite. If it's indefinite, there is no need to use a relative pronoun as the two sentences connect without a pronoun. Consider the following examples.

1 **shuft binit kaanat til3ab faTbool.**
   I saw a girl playing football.
2 **3ndi mushkilih kbiirih ma sharikat ilinternit.**
   I have a big problem with the internet company.

Exercise 10

Use *illi* wherever needed. If there is no need, just write 0.

1 ishtareyt sayyaarah jdiidih _____ baruuH fiiha 3aljaam3ah.
2 maktabit iljaam3ah _____ kunt ?adrus fiiha Hilwah kthiir.
3 ilmadiinih _____ baHibha hiiyih shiikagu.
4 jaam3it haarvard _____ aHsan jaam3ah.
5 ?akil maama _____ 3imlatuh zaaki (delicious) kthiir.

The past tense

The past tense in Arabic is made from the root verb; refer to the Introduction for a brief discussion of root morphology. Verb roots in Arabic are the default forms, meaning all other derivations stem from them. The root meaning is always associated with two other elements: indication of the past along with third person singular (he) as the "default" doer of the action in the verb. Table 7.4 gives some examples:

Table 7.4 Root forms

	Root	Past tense	Meaning
1	d+r+s	daras	he studied
2	?+k+l	?akal	he ate
3	sh+r+b	sharib	he drank
4	3+r+f	3araf	he knew
5	s+m+H	samaH	he allowed
6	k+t+b	katab	he wrote
7	3+r+r+f	3arraf	he introduced
8	gh+l+l+b	ghallab	he bothered
9	3+T+T+l	3aTTal	he took a vacation/leave
10	?+sh+t+r	?ishtara	he bought

The roots do not have vowels in them. Some roots have either a 'w' or a 'y' but these are not the vowel versions. Notice that the vowel pattern in the past is mostly **a-a** but can be different sometimes.

Now, let's consider the past tense derivations with the different pronouns. I will use the verb /**katab**/ to present these forms. Table 7.5 shows the past tense with all pronouns used in LA.

Table 7.5 Past tense **(Audio 2.18)**

Pronoun		Past tense	English
ana	I	**katabit**	I wrote
iHna	we	**katabna**	We wrote
intih	you (sing. masc.)	**katabit**	You (sing. masc.) wrote
inti	you (sing. fem.)	**katabti**	You (sing. fem.) wrote
intu	you (pl. masc.)	**katabtu**	You (pl. masc.) wrote
intin	you (pl. fem.)	**katabtin**	You (pl. fem.) wrote
huu	he	**katab**	He wrote
hii	she	**katbat**	She wrote
hummih	they (pl. masc.)	**katabu**	They (pl. masc.) wrote
hinnih	they (pl. fem.)	**katabu/katabin**	They (pl. fem.) wrote

Keep in mind that Arabic does not have a word for "it." All non-human or inanimate subjects are assigned a gender and therefore referred to by either "he" or "she." Plural inanimate nouns are treated in terms of gender and number agreement such as feminine singular.

Exercise 11

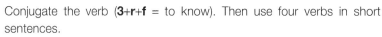

Conjugate the verb (**3+r+f** = to know). Then use four verbs in short sentences.

Pronoun		Past tense	English
ana	I	_____	_____
iHna	we	_____	_____
intih	you (sing. masc.)	_____	_____
inti	you (sing. fem.)	_____	_____
intu	you (pl. masc.)	_____	_____
intin	you (pl. fem.)	_____	_____
huu	he	_____	_____
hii	she	_____	_____
hummih	they (pl. masc.)	_____	_____
hinnih	they (pl. fem.)	_____	_____

Exercise 12 (Bonus audio 25)

If you have the audio, listen to the words and phrases, repeat and write them down.

Unit Eight

حياة الجامعة

Hayaat iljaam3ah

University life

In this unit, you will learn about:

- University life
- Fields of study
- Transportation
- Demonstratives
- Present and future tense

University life

Arab universities are similar in many ways to Western systems of higher education. Students finish high school and then submit applications for different universities. Nevertheless, the selection criteria vary from one country to another and within the same country. In most Arab countries, there are different quotas for admission. These quotas have developed to benefit the sons and daughters of employees who have performed certain services in the public sector. For example, in Jordan, the children of army veterans, university employees, judges and teachers in public schools make use of quotas in public universities that give them priority over others in admission under certain circumstances. Therefore, the student body in any given university in Jordan is diverse, i.e., it tends to have sizeable numbers of students from diverse backgrounds. Countries in the Levant, especially Jordan and Lebanon, are home to large numbers of students from different Arab countries.

In recent years, an increasing level of violence has made its way onto university campuses. Reasons continue to be under investigation, but often violence is sparked by protests against fees, grading systems and general rivalry between students from different social backgrounds. There can also sometimes be limited demonstrations inside university campuses in relation to regional conflicts, especially those having to do with the Palestinian–Israeli conflict. In most cases, however, these acts of violence are limited in terms of scope and results.

That said, one should remember that university campuses are generally very safe. Almost all universities are closed campuses: one cannot enter a university campus without a university ID card or without an escort. Almost all universities have security departments manned by police and army veterans.

Fields of study

Table 8.1 gives the most common fields of study at universities.

Table 8.1 University majors **(Audio 2.19)**

LA	English	LA	English
Tibb	Medicine	**igtiSaad**	Economics
Tibb asnaan	Dentistry	**muHaasabih**	Accounting
handasih	Engineering	**tamwiil**	Finance
Saydalih	Pharmacy	**taswiiq**	Marketing
tamriiDH	Nursing	**idaarah 3aamih**	Public administration
Haasuub	Computing	**ingiliizi**	English language
riyaaDHiyaat	Math	**3arabi**	Arabic language
fiizya	Physics	**faransi**	French language
kiimya	Chemistry	**sharii3ah**	Sharia
ʔaHyaa	Biology	**taariix**	History
jiiloojya	Geology	**jughraafya**	Geography
ziraa3ah	Agriculture	**tarbiyih**	Education
miyaah	Water resources	**siyaaHah**	Tourism
taghthyih	Nutrition	**riyaaDHah**	Physical education

Dialogue 1 **(Audio 2.20–2.21)**

Hiba and Amani talk about their majors.

HIBA: kiifik amaani? shuu btidursi?
AMAANI: hala hiba. ana badrus fiizya.
HIBA: ilfiizya Sa3bih. allaah y3iinik.
AMAANI: bass ana baHibb ilfiizya. w inti shuu taxaSSuSik?
HIBA: ana taxaSSuSi tamriiD.
AMAANI: kamaan ittamriiD Sa3b w Tawiil.
HIBA: bass ishshughul mawjuud ba3d ittaxarruj.
AMAANI: SaHiiH. allaah ywafgik.
HIBA: w inti kamaan.

Vocabulary

Sa3b	difficult
y3iinik (3+w+n)	to help, to support
taxaSSuS (pl. taxaSSuSaat)	specialization
Tawiil	tall, long, takes a long time
shughul	work
mawjuud	available
taxarruj (t+x+x+r+j)	graduation
SaHiiH	correct, right
ywafgik (w+f+g)	to help achieve one's goals

New expressions

allaah y3iinik: lit., may Allah support you. An expression used to wish help and support for someone.

allaah ywafqik: lit., may Allah help you. An expression used to wish someone help and success in achieving his/her goals.

Exercise 1

What do you think would be the university major of each of the following people?

1 Albert Einstein
2 Thomas Edison
3 Mother Teresa
4 Barack Obama
5 Bashar Assad
6 Sir Alexander Fleming
7 Marie Curie
8 Ahmed Zewail
9 Nagib Mahfouz
10 Martin Luther King

Exercise 2

Fill in the blanks with the appropriate word from the box.

Sa3bah	taxaSSuS	Tawiilih	shughul
mawjuudih	ʔattxarraj	SaHiiH	

1 kull innaas biHibbu _____ iTTibb.
2 diraasit ilhandasih _____ mithil diraasit iTTibb.
3 fiih taxaSSuSSaat kthiir _____ fi iljaam3ah ilurduniiyih.
4 mish kull innaas bilaagu (find) _____ kwayyis.
5 uxti 3indha mushkilih _____ kthiir.
6 lamma _____ min iljaam3ah, laazim adrus fii bariTaanyia.

  Dialogue 2 **(Audio 2.22–2.23)**

Omar and Sleiman talk about their daily schedule.

3UMAR: sleymaan, shuu 3indak ilyoom?
SLEYMAAN:. ahleyn 3umar, ilyoom fiih 3indi thalaath muHaaDHaraat
           wara ba3DH.
3UMAR: wall! thalaath wara ba3DH? kthiir heyk.
SLEYMAAN: bi3iin allaah. w intih shuu 3indak?
3UMAR: muHaaDHarteyn. bass waHdih ma3 duktoor jdiid, ma
           ba3rafuh.
SLEYMAAN: in shaa allaah yiTla3 kwayyis.
3UMAR: in shaa allaah. mata naawi titghadda?
SLEYMAAN: issaa3ah thinteyn 3indi faraagh.
3UMAR: xalaS, ghadaak ilyoom 3ala Hsaabi.
SLEYMAAN: shukran, shukran.
3UMAR: waajibna.
SLEYMAAN: allaah ysallmak.

Vocabulary

wara	behind
ba3DH	some
heyk	this/for this reason
bi3iin (3+w+n)	to help
yiTla3	to become; to turn out to be
naawi (n+w+y)	to intend to, to plan to
titghadda (gh+d+d)	to have lunch
faraagh (pl. faraaghaat)	free time
ghada	lunch
Hsaab (pl. Hsaabaat)	account
waajib (pl. waajibaat)	duty
ysallmak (s+l+l+m)	to keep (one) at peace

New expressions

wara ba3DH: back to back. This expression is used to describe events or objects that are adjacent to each other or that occur one right after another.

Haay issanih fiih 3uTliteyn wara ba3DH.
This year there are two holidays/vacations back to back.

wall!: an expression used to indicate one's surprise and astonishment. It's more commonly used to express surprise at bad events. Sometimes, the vowel can be lengthened as in /**baaal**/.

Someone just told you about a terrible accident in which many people passed away. You say:

wall! kullhum maatu?
Wow! All of them passed away?

kthiir heyk: this is too much. One can also say /**galiil heyk**/ to express the opposite. These two expressions can be used in negotiating prices as well as expressing that something is taking too long, or too short a time.

bi3iin allaah: An expression of solidarity, reassuring someone that help and support are there.

fiih nuSS malyoon laaji? fi ilurdun.	**bi3iin allaah**
there are half a million refugees in Jordan	May God help!

xalaS: enough, done. Sometimes, this expression can mean "enough, no more." It can sometimes be used to seal an agreement and avoid further discussion.

3ala Hsaabi: it's my treat. This is a very common expression used in cafés and restaurants. When friends are finished with their food or drink, the one who wants to pay says this to pay for all the others. Usually, the offer is contested by someone who insists on paying.

allaah ysallmak: lit., may Allah keep you safe. This expression can be used on a number of occasions: if one returns from a trip, as an answer to a leave-taking expression, or as a thank-you expression.

Exercise 3

Translate Dialogue 2 above. Use the vocabulary list and your under-standing of the context. Avoid using a dictionary.

Transportation

Most students commute to universities using public transportation. The cheapest and most popular type are mid-size buses. These buses have fixed routes. They pick up students from different villages, towns and edges of big cities to university campuses. Some students commute for more than 200 km every day. More often than not, these buses are crowded and students have to fight to get a seat, especially during rush hour.

Dialogue 3 (Audio 2.24)

Uthman and Khalil are waiting for the university bus.

3UTHMAAN:	mTawwil ilbaaS, ya axi? shaklna raH nit?axxar.
XALIIL:	mish 3aarif. in shaa allaah yuuSal bsur3ah.
3UTHMAAN:	ilyoom ?azmih kbiirih. laazim nilHag makaan bilbaaS.

XALIIL: saHiiH. bass maa ba3rif idha bnliHag makaan ma3
haay il?azmih.
3UTHMAAN: isma3 ya xaliil, bass yiiji ilbaaS, intih btiTla3 min
ishshubbaak.
XALIIL: leysh aTla3 min ishshubbaak?
3UTHMAAN: 3alashaan tiHjiz illi w ilak.
XALIIL: fikrah mumtaazih, 3ala Tuul.
3UTHMAAN: bass maa ti3Ti ilkursi la ?awwal binit.
XALIIL: la, la, maa ba3malha. ma txaaf.
3UTHMAAN: ba3irfak niswanji.
XALIIL: allaah ysaamHak.

Vocabulary

mTawwil (T+w+l)	taking it/him a long time to (arrive)
baaS (pl. baaSaat)	bus
raH	will
nit?axxar (?+x+x+r)	to be late; to come late
yuuSal (w+S+l)	to arrive
sur3ah	fast
?azmih (pl. ?azmaat)	traffic jam; crowded
nilHag (l+H+g)	to catch (a bus, someone, an appointment)
makaan (pl. amaakin)	place
idha	if
isma3 (s+m+3)	to hear
yiiji (j+?+y)	to come; to arrive
shubbaak (pl. shababiik)	window
leysh	why
3alashaan	because
tiHjiz (H+j+z)	to reserve
ti3Ti (3+T+y)	to give
kursi (pl. karaasi)	chair
ba3malha (3+m+l)	to do; to make
txaaf (x+w+f)	to fear
niswanji	womanizer; loves women
ysaamiH (s+m+H)	to forgive

New expressions

shaklna: shakl+na: lit., shape + we: our shape. This is a noun that is usually attached to a relative pronoun. It means "it seems that we", "it seems that he", etc. depending on the pronoun attached. Though it is a noun phrase, it gives the meaning of "it seems that."

> **maa fiih baaS la iljaam3ah ilyoon. shakil raH at?axxar.**
> There is no bus to university today. It seems I will be late.

niswanji: adj., womanizer. This expression is used to describe someone who loves to hang around women, or loves to talk to them as opposed to socializing with men.

> **ishshabaab maa biHibbu ay waaHad niswanji.**
> The guys do not like anyone who's a womanizer.

allaah ysaamHak: may Allah forgive you. This expression is used to ask for forgiveness for someone. Sometimes, as in this context, it's used as a polite way of defending oneself against an accusation.

 ## Exercise 4

Using information from Dialogues 1–3 in this unit, write adjectives that seem to fit each of the following people. Explain your answers.

1 Amani
2 Omar
3 Sleiman
4 Khalil

Expressions

Notice the use of the following expressions. See how they are used in the context, too.

1 **maa ba3rif idha: maa ba3rfi idha 3indana imtiHaan.**
   I do not know if we have a test.
2 **ma3 haay: ma3 haay ilHaraarah, ma raH nigdar nisbaH.**
   With this temperature, we will not be able to swim.

3 **bass . . . , b . . . : bass tiwSal iljaam3ah, btiHki ma3i.**
When you arrive at the university, you call me.
4 **bass maa + verb: bass maa tishrab wiski.**
But do not drink whiskey.

Exercise 5

Use the following expressions in short sentences similar to the ways they're used above:

1 maa ba3rif idha
2 bass

3 ma3
4 bass . . . b . . .

Demonstratives (Audio 2.25)

Table 8.2 presents the most commonly used demonstrative pronouns in LA.

Table 8.2 Demonstratives in LA

	LA	English	Notes
1	**haadha; haaDH; haada; haad**	this (masc.)	use of DH is rural; associated with males
2	**haay; haathi; haadi**	this (fem.)	use of haathi is Bedouin
3	**haDHool; hadool; haathu; haadu**	these (masc., fem.)	
4	**haDHaak; hadaak,**	that (masc.)	
5	**haDHiik; hadiik**	that (fem.)	
6	**haDHoolaak; hadlaak**	those (masc., fem.)	

Exercise 6

Use the appropriate demonstrative in each of the following sentences.

1 _____ liktaab Tawiil w Sa3b.
2 shuuf, shuuf, _____ aHla binit fi iljaam3ah.
3 _____ sayyaatri. shuu ra?yak fiiha?
4 _____ ilustaadh daayman (always) bis?alni ana bass.
5 _____ ilmaT3am illi fi ?aaxir ishshaari3 ?akluh mumtaaz.

Present and future tense

Present and future tenses in LA are identical. Expressing future in LA is not performed on the verb. Rather, it is expressed using a future adverb of time, or with the help of a future time indication. Sometimes, a particle /**raH**/, meaning "will," precedes the present verb to indicate future. Table 8.3 presents verbs in the present tense with all pronouns in LA.

Table 8.3 Present tense

Pronoun		Present tense	English
ana	I	**baktub/baktib**	I write
iHna	we	**bnuktub/bniktib**	We write
intih	you (sing. masc.)	**btuktub/btiktib**	You (sing. masc.) write
inti	you (sing. fem.)	**btukutbi/btikitbi**	You (sing. fem.) write
intu	you (pl. masc.)	**btukutbu/btikitbu**	You (pl. masc.) write
intin	you (pl. fem.)	**btukutbin/btikitbin**	You (pl. fem.) write
huu	he	**buktub/biktib**	He writes
hii	she	**btuktub/btiktib**	She writes
hummih	they (pl. masc.)	**bikutbu/biktibu**	They (pl. masc.) write
hinnih	they (pl. fem.)	**bikutbin/bikitbin**	They (pl. fem.) write

To express the future tense simply add /**raH**/ or /**bid**/+corresponding pronoun before the verb. See the following examples:

1 **ana raH asaafir 3ala maSr bukrah.**
   I will travel to Egypt tomorrow.
2 **xawla raH titzawwaj ba3d shahr.**
   Khawla will get married in a month.
3 **iHna bidna nil3ab sallih.**
   We will play basketball.
4 **ana maa biddi aakul ?akl Siini.**
   I do not want to eat Chinese food.

Exercise 7

Read the following story. Underline the words that seem to be wrong. Write a better answer.

ʔaS3ab shii innuh tidrus kull yoom li arba3 sanih w ba3deyn maa kaanat fiih shughul. ya3ni shuu bilaazim ni3mal 3alashaan ʔalaagi shughul? bidna maSaari. mish mumkin nuTlub maSaari fi ahilna ba3d ma ykuun ilwaaHad minna 3umrhum thneyn w 3ishriin sniin. ana mumkin yishtaghil ay shii wala akuun fi ilbeyt daayman naayimaat. ba3deyn biduun shughul, keyf bidna nitzawwaj?

Exercise 8 (Bonus audio 28)

If you have the audio, listen to the words and phrases, repeat and write them down.

Unit Nine

في السوق
fi issuug

At the market

In this unit, you will learn about:

- The Arab souk
- Bargaining
- Cultural awareness
- Imperatives
- Negation of verbs
- Cause and effect

Arab souk

Shopping in the Arab world is gradually yielding to globalization. In many places in major cities, shopping malls are beginning to sprout up. The shopping experience in these places is not much different from other similar places around the world. There can still be some variation in the types of goods offered, or the kinds of food available, but a more authentic shopping experience continues to exist in old markets still resisting the wave of globalization. These markets are usually found in the older quarters of major Arab cities. This is a unique experience in most major cities in the Arab world. The best place to look for such an experience is the "old madinah" of any major Arab town. This is usually the heart of the town, where you are likely to find stores that date back hundreds of years.

Visiting these places is part and parcel of trying to understand the soul of the Arab city. You are likely to find craftsmen of many types, authentic food, different types of desserts, old-time cafés, tailors, carpenters, blacksmiths, etc. The learning experiences these places offer are truly priceless.

Bargaining

Shopping in big malls strips this skill from people since prices are fixed and there is no room for bargaining. Shopping in smaller stores is where the true experience lies. If you are shopping for clothes, jewelry, souvenirs, collectibles or gifts, it's likely that these items will be overpriced. The reason is that rarely does anyone pay the price that the seller asks for at first. Once the seller says the prices, negotiations begin. Sometimes, this will be a fast exchange: the seller asks for a given price, the buyer gives a very low counter offer, which results in the seller going away and not even discussing the deal. But more often than not, the buyer will offer a lower price, the seller asks for a higher price explaining how the merchandise is worth it and that it is a very good deal. Eventually, both agree and the deal is sealed.

But how do people bargain? In most cases, it is wise to offer 30 per cent less than the asking price. The seller will then insist on 5–15 per cent off and might eventually agree to 20 per cent off. A good rule of thumb is to ask about the price of what you want to buy in different places so as to get an idea about the approximate asking price. The next step is to show that you're not desperate for the merchandise and to say that you can get it in other places. If the seller sticks to his/her offer, then walk away. This usually forces many sellers to agree to sell to a much lower price compared to their first offer. But at any rate, make sure you maintain the respect of the seller and thank him/her even if you walk away without closing a deal.

 Dialogue 1 (Audio 2.26)

 John walks into a gift store. He wants to buy a gift for his mother. Omar, the store keeper, tries to close the deal with him.

JOON:	marHaba.
3UMAR:	ahlan wa sahlan, itfaDDal?
JOON:	idha samaHt, biddi ?ashtari shaal w xaatim fiDDah la ummi.
3UMAR:	3ala Tuul. shuu loon ishshaal?
JOON:	mish 3aarif, shuu 3indak alwaan?
3UMAR:	fiih aHmar, abyaD, aswad, azrag, bunni, ramaadi, beij, zahri, aSfar, kuHli.
JOON:	la la, ma biddiish saada. biddi mzarkash: aHmar ma3 abyaD, aswad 3ala aSfar.
3UMAR:	aah, maashi. haay aHmar ma3 abyaD, aswad ma3 aSfar, azrag ma3 zahri.
JOON:	ilazraq ma3 izzahri Hilu.
3UMAR:	SaHiiH, haadha Hilu ktiir.
JOON:	Tayyib, mumkin ashuuf ilxawaatim?
3UMAR:	3ala raasi. haadha xaatim fiDDah ?aSli. bass ghaali shwai.
JOON:	mumkin ashuuf waaHad thaani?
3UMAR:	3ala Tuul. haadha waaHad thaani.
JOON:	iththaani aHsan. bikamm ishshaal wil xaatim?
3UMAR:	iliththneyn bi xamsih w sittiin diinaar, 3alashaanak bass.
JOON:	xamsih w sittiin? la kthir heyk. shuu ra?yak bi xamsiin?
3UMAR:	la mish mumkin, raas maaluh xamsiin. mumkin bi sittiin.
JOON:	lissa kthiir ghaali. ana akthar min xamsih w xamsiin maa ma3i.
3UMAR:	maashi ya sidi, itfaDDal.
JOON:	shukran ya sidi.
3UMAR:	ahlan wa sahlan, mabrook, ma3 issalaamih.

Vocabulary

ʔashtari (sh+t+r)	to buy
shaal (pl. shaalaat)	scarf
xaatim (pl. xawaatim)	ring
fiDDah (n.)	silver
loon (pl. alwaan)	color
saada (adj.)	one color
mzarkash (adj.)	embroidered
ʔaSli (adj.)	original
ghaali (adj.)	expensive
aHsan (adj.)	better
3alashaan	because
ray+ak	your opinion
raas maal	prime cost
lissa	yet
mabrook/mubaarak	congratulations

New expressions

saada: of colors, means a single color; not two or more mixed colors.

mzarkash: embroidered. This refers to mixing colors in one garment.

aswad 3ala/ma3 aSfar: black on yellow.

3alashaanak bass: lit., just for you. This expression is heavily used when someone wants to sell you something. It's said during bargaining when the seller wants to lock down the price. Some people also use it when they do you a favor.

shuu raʔyak?: what do you think? Asking one's opinion.

raas maaluh: lit., its capital. This term is used by sellers to convince buyers that they're not making much profit, or not making profit at all. It is mostly a strategy to lock down a deal.

Exercise 1

Translate Dialogue 1 above. Use the vocabulary list and your understanding of the context. Try to avoid using a dictionary.

Dialogue 2 (Audio 2.27–2.28)

Mark wants to buy trousers and a shirt. He walks into a clothing
store.

MAARK:	masaa? ilxeyr Hajji.
SHOP OWNER:	masaa? innuur. ahlan wa sahlan. tfaDDal 3ammi.
MAARK:	badawwir 3ala gamiiS w banTaloon.
SHOP OWNER:	mawjuud. shuu ilmudeyl illi bitHibuh?
MAARK:	biddi banTaloon jiinz w gamiiS kwayyis.
SHOP OWNER:	haay jiinz aswad, w haay azrag. w haay gamiiS saada
	w fiih mgallam.
MAARK:	ilbanTaloon azrag idha mumkin. w ilgamiiS mgallam.
SHOP OWNER:	tfaDDal, heyk kwayyis?
MAARK:	mumtaaz. bass haadha Sghiir. ana balbis sittih w
	thalaathiin w ilgamiiS laarj.
SHOP OWNER:	maashi ya sidi. tfaDDal, haay gyaasak.
MAARK:	tamaam. bkam haDDool Hajji?
SHOP OWNER:	3ala Hsaabak. bala maSaari.
MAARK:	allaah ybaarik fiik. bkam? bass raa3iina.
SHOP OWNER:	3alashaanak bxamsih w thalaathiin diinaar.
MAARK:	xamsih w thalaathiin? kthiir heyk. w ana Taalib.
SHOP OWNER:	bass haaDHa guTin ?aSli, mish Siini wala suuri.
MAARK:	bass wallah kthiir. shuu ra?yak bixamsih w 3shriin?
SHOP OWNER:	laa mish mumkin. thalaathiin ?aaxir si3ir.
MAARK:	thalaathiin maashi. tfaDDal.
SHOP OWNER:	shukran. mabruuk.
MAARK:	shukran Hajji.
SHOP OWNER:	ma3 issalaamih.

Vocabulary

badawwir 3ala (d+w+w+r)	to look for; search for
mudeyl (pl. mudeylaat)	fashion; style
banTaloon (pl. banaTiil)	trousers, pants
jiinz	jeans
mgallam	striped
balbis (l+b+s)	to wear
laarj	large
gyaas (pl. gyaasaat)	size
maSaari	money
raa3ii (r+3+y)	to take care of someone
guTin	cotton
Siini	Chinese
suuri	Syrian
si3ir or thaman	price

New expressions

heyk kwayyis: lit., this is good. This is used when one likes an arrangement or a deal.

3ala Hsaabak: lit., on your account. This is a common expression of generosity. In this context, the shop owner politely offers his merchandise for free. But this is strictly an expression of respect and generosity. It does not mean that he is really willing to do so. So, it would be very inappropriate to accept the offer.

bala maSaari: without money. This is similar to the previous expression. It's an offer to take the merchandise for free. Just like before, the proper response is to thank the person and insist on paying the price. Notice that negotiations are fine but taking something for free is not.

?aTaani ilgamiiS bala maSaari.
He gave me the shirt without money (for free).

raa3iina: lit., take care of us. An expression used to push the seller to reduce his/her asking price.

Exercise 2

Write a short dialogue in which you use the four expressions outlined above. Write the setting of the dialogue in English first.

Exercise 3a

Match words from column 1 with words from column 2. Then use them in sentences.

Column 1		*Column 2*	
1	ʔashtari	a	maaluh
2	shaal	b	Hsaabak
3	walad	c	niswanji
4	gamiiS	d	saada
5	xaatim	e	raʔyak
6	raas	f	baTaloon
7	loon	g	guTun
8	bala	h	mzarkash
9	3ala	i	fiDDah
10	shuu	j	maSaari

Exercise 3b

Now use them to make ten short sentences.

Imperatives (Audio 2.29)

Imperatives are verbs that require someone to do something. In LA, this verb is formed in the present since the occurrence of the verb, should it appear, takes place in the future. Imperatives are always in the second person, i.e., using variations of the second person pronoun: you. Table 9.1 introduces imperatives.

Table 9.1 Imperatives

Pronoun		Imperative	English
intih	you (sing. masc.)	**uktub**	You (sing. masc.) write
inti	you (sing. fem.)	**uktubi**	You (sing. fem.) write
intu	you (pl. masc.)	**uktubu**	You (pl. masc.) write
intin	you (pl. fem.)	**uktubin**	You (pl. fem.) write

Exercise 4

Change each of the following sentences into the imperative. See the example:

Example:
aHmad daras handasih.   ya aHmad, udrus handasih.

1 3umar ishtara ktbaab.
2 leyla shaafat film jdiid.
3 iHna ʔakalna falaafil.
4 ilizabith raaHat 3ala iddukkaan.
5 toom li3ib riyaaDah.

Negation of verbs

LA uses two particles for negation of verbs depending on the tense and the completion of the action denoted by the verb. Here are the rules for negation of each of the tenses:

Past: maa+verb+(-sh)
Present: maa+verb+-(-sh)
Future: maa+raH+verb
           mish+raH+verb

Tables 9.2–9.4 give negation forms with the root /**k**+**t**+**b**/ and all pronouns.

Table 9.2 Negation – past tense

Pronoun		Past tense	Negation	English
ana	I	**katabit**	**maa katabt(ish)**	I didn't write
iHna	we	**katabna**	**maa katabna(ash)**	We didn't write
intih	you (sing. masc.)	**katabit**	**maa katabit**	You (sing. masc.) didn't write
inti	you (sing. fem.)	**katabti**	**maa katabti(ish)**	You (sing. fem.) didn't write
intu	you (pl. masc.)	**katabtu**	**maa katabtu(ush)**	You (pl. masc.) didn't write
intin	you (pl. fem.)	**katabtin**	**maa katabtin(nish)**	You (pl. fem.) didn't write
huu	he	**katab**	**maa katab(ish)**	He didn't write
hii	she	**katbat**	**maa katbat(ish)**	She didn't write
hummih	they (pl. masc.)	**katabu**	**maa katabu(ush)**	They (pl. masc.) didn't write
hinnih	they (pl. fem.)	**katabu/ katabin**	**maa katabu(ush) maa katabin(-nish)**	They (pl. fem.) didn't write

Table 9.3 Negation – present tense

Pronoun		Present tense	Negation	English
ana	I	**baktub** **baktib**	**maa baktub(ish)** **maa baktib(ish)**	I don't write
iHna	we	**bnuktub** **bniktib**	**maa bnuktub(ish)** **maa bniktib(ish)**	We don't write
intih	you (sing. masc.)	**btuktub** **btiktib**	**maa btuktub(ish)** **maa btiktib(ish)**	You (sing. masc.) don't write
inti	you (sing. fem.)	**btukutbi** **btikitbi**	**maa btukutbi(ish)** **maa btikitbi(ish)**	You (sing. fem.) don't write
intu	you (pl. masc.)	**btukutbu** **btikitbu**	**maa btukutbu(ush)** **maa btikitbu(ush)**	You (pl. masc.) don't write
intin	you (pl. fem.)	**btukutbin** **btikitbin**	**maa btukutbin(nish)** **maa btikitbin(nish)**	You (pl. fem.) don't write
huu	he	**buktub** **biktib**	**maa buktub(ish)** **maa biktib(ish)**	He doesn't write
hii	she	**btuktub** **btiktib**	**maa btuktub(ish)** **maa btiktib(ish)**	She doesn't write
hummih	they (pl. masc.)	**bikutbu** **biktibu**	**maa bikutbu(ush)** **maa biktibu(ush)**	They (pl. masc.) don't write
hinnih	they (pl. fem.)	**bikutbin** **bikitbin**	**maa bikutbin(nish)** **maa bikitbin(nish)**	They (pl. fem.) don't write

Table 9.4 Negation – future tense

Pronoun		Future tense	Negation	English
ana	I	**raH aktub**	maa/mish raH aktub	I won't write
		raH aktib	maa/mish raH aktib	
iHna	we	**raH nuktub**	maa/mish raH nuktub	We won't write
		raH niktib	maa/mish raH niktib	
intih	you (sing. masc.)	**raH tuktub**	maa/mish raH tuktub	You (sing. masc.) won't write
		raH tiktib	maa/mish raH tiktib	
inti	you (sing. fem.)	**raH tukutbi**	maa/mish raH tukutbi	You (sing. fem.) won't write
		raH tikitbi	maa/mish raH tikitbi	
intu	you (pl. masc.)	**raH tukutbu**	maa/mish raH tukutbu	You (pl. masc.) won't write
		raH tikitbu	maa/mish raH tikitbu	
intin	you (pl. fem.)	**raH tukutbin**	maa/mish raH tukutbin	You (pl. fem.) won't write
		raH tikitbin	maa/mish raH tikitbin	
huu	he	**raH yuktub**	maa/mish raH yuktub	He won't write
		raH yiktib	maa/mish raH yiktib	
hii	she	**raH tuktub**	maa/mish raH tuktub	She won't write
		raH tiktib	maa/mish raH tiktib	
hummih	they (pl. masc.)	**raH yukutbu**	maa/mish raH yukutbu	They (pl. masc.) won't write
		raH yiktibu	maa/mish raH yiktibu	
hinnih	they (pl. fem.)	**raH yukutbin**	maa/mish raH yukutbin	They (pl. fem.) won't write
		raH yikitbin	maa/mish raH yikitbin	

Exercise 5

Negate the following sentences. Make sure you use different forms of negation. Notice that you can negate different items in the sentence and give a different meaning. See the example first:

Example:
3indi muHaaDHarah ma3 duktoor jdiid.

A. *maa* **3indi muHaaDHarah ma3 duktoor jdiid.**
I do not have a class with new professor.

B. **3nidi muHaaDHarah ma3 duktoor *mish* jdiid.**
I have a class with a professor who's not new.

1 fikrah mumtaazih.
2 i3Ti xaalid xams danaaniir.
3 ʔamiiSik haada Hilu.
4 ana baHibb illoon ilaxDar.

5 mumkin ykuun mitluh fi ilurdun.
6 bukrah raH adrus 3ashr saa3aat.
7 haadha xaatim fiDDah ʔaSli.
8 biddi banTaloon jiinz.
9 allaah ybaarik fiik.
10 bass wallah kthiir.

Exercise 6

Respond to each of the following questions or statements using negation. Write full sentences:

1 bti3rafi ti3mali mansaf?
2 haadha ilbanTaloon bi arb3iin diinaar.
3 iljaw kwayyis ilyoom?
4 3indak sayyaarah fi amriika?
5 mumkin tishtarii li biitza?
6 ishrab kamaan shay.

Cause and effect

In LA, cause and effect expressions are formed through the use of /**3alashaan**/ or the shorter form /**3ashaan**/ meaning "for" or "because." Sometimes, another connector (/**li** +**ʔann**/+ pronoun) is used.
    Consider the following examples:

1 **3alashaan anjaH laazmi adrus.**
    In order to succeed, I have to study.
2 **biddi arooH bsur3ah 3ashaan alHag ilmuHaaDHarah.**
    I want to go fast so that I can catch the lecture.
3 **ishtraeyt haay issayyaarah 3ashnha jdiidih.**
    I bought this car because it is new.
4 **laʔinha Sghiirih, ba3dha bti3mal mashaakil.**
    Because she is young, she continues to make problems.
5 **maa ʔakalna laʔinnuh ilʔakil kaan mish Hilu.**
    We did not eat because the food was not sweet.

In some Syrian dialects **kirmaal** كرمال is used instead. /**3alashaan**/ or its shorter form are more commonly used than /**kirmaal**/.

Exercise 7

Translate each of the following sentences from English into LA. Make sure to use cause/effect expressions.

1 I have to go to Amman for a lecture.
2 Because the tea was not good, I did not drink it.
3 I don't eat chicken because I'm vegetarian.
4 To be able to go to the restaurant, I have to leave now.
5 I must go back to England to see my mother.

Exercise 8

Study each of the following sentences, and then change them as required.

1 **nabiilah raaHat 3ala issuug imbaariH.**
   a Past
   b Present
   c Negation
   d Present + negation
2 **xaalid w salma bidursu Tibb fi iljaam3ah ilamriikiyyih.**
   a Past
   b Future
   c Negation
   d Past + negation
3 **laazim ?ashtari talifoon jdiid.**
   a Past
   b Negation
   c Present + negation

Exercise 9 (Bonus audio 31)

If you have the audio, listen to the words and phrases, repeat and write them down.

Cultural point

Shopping for clothes can be a very interesting experience. Depending on where you choose to shop, you might end up paying more or less money for almost the same type of merchandise. It is always wise to buy with a group of people rather than going on your own. The idea is that the retailer is tempted to give you a good deal if there is a chance that more items will be purchased or some of your company might also decide to buy. Brand names are a big selling point but more often than not, do not trust the brands as many are actually fake. Once you start negotiating prices, you will notice that world famous brands are sold for cheap prices. This is because they are imitations of the original brands. However, some major retailers do sell the original brands. In these places, there is usually no room for bargaining since each price is marked and the retailer has no freedom to change it.

Bargaining prices requires some training. In some places, especially where traditional, heritage and ethnic merchandise is sold, prices can vary considerably. The first thing to do is to shop around first and get an idea of the price range. This is usually a very good strategy that enables you to get a very good idea of the actual value. But also different countries have different practices. For example, many Syrian retailers usually ask for more than double the actual price and then go down as you negotiate. So if you offer them half the price they ask for, this can be a very good point to begin the negotiations. On the other hand, the great majority of Jordanian retailers do not go below 20 or 30 per cent of the asking price and if you try to cut them down for half the asking price, many of them will simply walk away. Finally, bargaining and price negotiations are common in small family businesses or small retailers, which are very common in the Middle East. Major retailers and big stores have no room for negotiations. However, they do announce several price reductions and you can find very good deals in them.

Unit Ten

المدينة العربية

ilmadiinih il3arabiyyih

The Arab town

In this unit, you will learn about:

- Going around the city
- Safety and security
- Important places and services
- Nominal sentences
- Verbal sentences

Going around the city

As mentioned in earlier units, cities have a lot to offer. In most Arab
countries, services in the major cities are much more abundant compared to services in smaller towns and villages. Among the best ways
to explore the city safely is to know major landmarks. While people
know the names of major streets, side streets in smaller quarters
of the city are not known to most people, but they can be easily
identified by knowing the names of major landmarks in those areas.
Use of GPS is also very limited since most cities in the Arab world
are not codified for use in these systems. But people are very helpful
when asked for directions.

 Dialogue 1 **(Audio 2.30–2.31)**

 John is trying to get to the clinic. He does not know where it is
and is asking a bystander.

JOON:	marHaba ya abu ishshabaab, mumkin suʔaal?
BYSTANDER:	ahleyn 3ammi, itfaDDal.
JOON:	weyn markiz ilʔamal iSSiHi?
BYSTANDER:	eyy, mish 3aarif bizzabT weyn, weyn galluulak?
JOON:	janb makkah mool. bass ana mish 3aarif weyn makkah mool.
BYSTANDER:	aah, makkah mool 3ala ʔaaxir ishshaari3.
JOON:	dughri?
BYSTANDER:	ruuH dughri la ʔaaxir ishshaari3, bilaagiik maHal blaly steyshin, waraah 3ala izzaawyih.
JOON:	ya3ni ʔaxxir ishshaari3, ba3deyn 3ala izzaawyih.
BYSTANDER:	tamaam, raayiH tlaagi 3amaarah kbiirih, yimkin ilmarkiz biTTaabig iththaalith aw irraabi3.
JOON:	shukran, baarak allaah fiik.
BYSTANDER:	hala 3ammi, ma3 issalaamih.

Vocabulary

suʔaal (pl. ʔasʔilih)	question
markiz (pl. maraakiz)	center
SiHi	healthy (markiz SiHi: health clinic)
bizzabT	exactly
galluulak (g+w+l)	to say; to tell
bilaagiik (l+g+y)	to find
maHal (pl. maHallaat)	store
bley steyshin	PlayStation
zaawyih (pl. zawaaya)	corner
Taabig (pl. Tawaabig)	floor
baarak (b+r+k)	to bless

New expressions

eyy: equivalent to English /mmm/, this expression is used to indicate hesitation, thinking before answering.

aah: equivalent to "I see." This expression is used when someone finds an answer to something.

baarak allaah fiik: may Allah give you bounty. A polite expression used to wish someone well.

hala 3ammi: lit., welcome uncle. This expression is equivalent to saying "you're welcome"; refer to the use of honorifics. If it is used with a rising tone, it could signal disagreement.

Exercise 1

Respond to each of the following situations using a short sentence. Make sure your sentence includes some of the new vocabulary and/or expressions.

1 **mumkin ti3Tiini thalthiin diinaar li ʔaaxir ishshahir?**
   You're hesistant to do so. After thinking for a short period of time, you say:

2 You forgot your phone on the dinner table. A man comes to you carrying it.
   You take it and respond saying:
3 Someone asked you about a place to have dinner.
   You're thinking about the best place and you just remembered one. You say:
4 A guest is at your place for the first time. He/she does not know where the bathroom is.
   Give him/her short directions.

Exercise 2

Dialogue 1 is copied below. Instead of John talking to a male bystander, imagine that Briana is asking a *female* bystander. Edit the dialogue accordingly.

JOON:	**marHaba ya abu ishshabaab, mumkin suʔaal?**
BRIANA:	_____
BYSTANDER:	**ahleyn 3ammi, itfaDDal.**
BYSTANDER:	_____
JOON:	**weyn markiz ilʔamal iSSiHi?**
BRIANA:	_____
BYSTANDER:	**eyy, mish 3aarif bizzabT weyn, weyn galluulak?**
BYSTANDER:	_____
JOON:	**janb makkah mool. bass ana mish 3aarif weyn makkah mool.**
BRIANA:	_____
BYSTANDER:	**aah, makkah mool 3ala ʔaaxir ishshaari3.**
BYSTANDER:	_____
JOON:	**dughri?**
BRIANA:	_____
BYSTANDER:	**ruuH dughri la ʔaaxir ishshaari3, bilaagiik maHal bley steyshin, waraah 3ala izzaawyih.**
JOON:	**ya3ni ʔaxxir ishshaari3, ba3deyn 3ala izzaawyih.**
BRIANA:	_____
BYSTANDER:	**tamaam, raayiH tlaagi 3amaarah kbiirih, yimkin ilmarkiz biTTaabig iththaalith aw irraabi3.**
BYSTANDER:	_____

JOON:	**shukran, baarak allaah fiik.**
BRIANA:	_____
BYSTANDER:	**hala 3ammi, ma3 issalaamih.**
BYSTANDER:	_____

Cultural point

Safety and security

As is the case in most places, safety and security in the Arab world is relative; some places are much safer than others. And some are safe during certain times of the day, but not so much at night, for example. Security is also different for men and women and also varies by age. Here are some general security tips:

- Avoid unwanted attention.
- Dress appropriately. Appropriate dress in the Arab world is trousers and shirts for men, long sleeves and trousers for women or long skirts that cover most of the body. Shorts and tank tops are not advisable. However, if one is on a university campus, dress code can be less rigid. Additionally, people are used to shorts and tank tops or bikinis in tourist places and beaches. This is generally a learning process. Over time, everyone can work out the proper dress.
- Avoid walking alone. Walking in groups is much safer.
- Avoid crowded places. These places often put people at the risk of being harassed or robbed.
- Keep your belongings safe and secure. There is no need to keep vital documents such as passports with you. You can use an ID card.
- Do not carry much cash around. Carry enough to get you by and keep your money in the bank or in a safe at the hotel.
- Stay connected. It's very easy to get a cell phone in all Arab countries and the service is very affordable.
- Keep phone numbers of some local friends handy. If you need immediate help, you can call them.

- Do not engage in heated discussions about religion and politics except with close friends and teachers or in an academic setting. Despite the fact that many people in the street can invite such discussions, it is wise to keep answers to a minimum, or to say that you're not interested in these issues.
- Avoid talking about or revealing your sexual orientation.
- People are generally very tolerant of Christians, but not so much of Jewish people or atheists. But in academic circles there is pretty much no problem.
- Finally, if you're in doubt, ask close friends or teachers. These people will always be some of your best resources.

Important places and services (Audio 2.32–2.33; Bonus audio 33)

When you arrive in a new country, there are several places that you will need for routine services. It is important to learn these places. Table 10.1 presents some of these.

Table 10.1 Important places and services

LA	English	LA	English
markiz shurTah	police station	**naadi**	club
maktab bariid	post office	**Sayydalliiyih**	pharmacy
safaarah	embassy	**muajjama3**	bus station
dukkaan/maHal	store or shop	**maHal xuDaar**	vegetable market
3iyaadih	clinic	**Saloon**	barber shop
mustashfa	hospital	**jaami3**	mosque
jim	gym	**kaniisih**	church
gahwah	café	**seynama**	cinema

Exercise 3

Use new vocabulary from this table to describe a problem that you faced to your friends. Talk about where you were, what happened, what you did, who was there, whether anyone helped you, etc. Be creative and use new vocabulary and grammar.

Dialogue 2 (Audio 2.34–2.35)

Sofia is telling her host mother about her weekly schedule.

HOST MOTHER:	soofia, shuu 3indik bukrah?
SOOFIA:	bukrah ya xaaltuh laazim ?aruuH 3ala il3iyaadih. 3indi waja3 asnaan.
HOST MOTHER:	salaamtik, ?ay 3iyaadih?
SOOFIA:	3iyaadit ilasnaan illi bjabal ittaaj.
HOST MOTHER:	aah, haay 3iyaadih mumtaazih. w ba3d bukrah?
SOOFIA:	ilmasaa fiih 3indi ijtimaa3 bissafaarah il?amriikiiyih
HOST MOTHER:	maashi. w yoom iliththneyn?
SOOFIA:	3indi muHaaDaraat kull ilyoom. bass il3aSr bidna nzuur masjid iljaam3ah ma3 iTTullaab.
HOST MOTHER:	kwayyis ktiir. yoom ittalaata maa 3indik shi?
SOOFIA:	3indi bass maw3id waaHid. laazim ?aruuH markiz ishshurTah ajaddid iqaamti.
HOST MOTHER:	in shaa allaah bitxallSi bsur3ah.
SOOFIA:	ilarbi3aa biddi ?ashtari fawaakih min maHal ilxuDaar.
HOST MOTHER:	ishtari min 3ind abu kariim. ilfawaakih illi 3induh Taaza.
SOOFIA:	bass mish ghaali shway? biddi maHal raxiiS.
HOST MOTHER:	ghaali, bass si3ruh fiih.
SOOFIA:	maashi. iljumm3ah mumkin ?aruuH 3ala iSSaloon a3mal sha3ri.
HOST MOTHER:	Hilu wallah. ana baruuH ma3ik.
SOOFIA:	bitsharrfi. yoom issabit, biddi aHDar filim ma3 SaaHbaati bil seynama.
HOST MOTHER:	fikrah Hilwah.
SOOFIA:	yoom ilaHad mitil ma bti3rafi laazim ?aruuH 3al kaniisih.

Vocabulary

waja3 (pl. awjaa3)	pain
sinn (pl. asnaan)	teeth
ʔay	which
jabal ittaaj	Jabal Altaaj (place name)
ijtimaa3 (pl. ijtimaa3aat)	meeting
3aSr	evening time
nzuur (z+aa+r)	to visit
maw3id (pl. mawaa3iid)	appointment
ajaddid (j+d+d)	to renew
iqaamah (pl. iqaamaat)	residency
xallSi (x+l+l+S)	to finish
fawaakih	fruit
xuDaar	vegetables
Taaza	fresh (food, drink)
raxiiS	cheap
sha3r	hair
aHDar (H+D+r)	to watch (a movie)
SaaHib (pl. SHaab)	friend (male)
SaaHbih (pl. SaaHbaat)	friend (female)

New expressions

3aSr: evening time. This is the name for the evening prayer. Arabs use this word to indicate time. You will see that many people make arrangements to meet using prayer times. The prayer times are: **fajr:** dawn; **DHuhr:** noontime; **3aSr:** evening time; **maghrib:** sunset; **3isha:** dinner time. Many people give appointments using **gabl** (before) or **ba3d** (after) followed by a prayer time.

Exercise 4

Write adjectives that can possibly describe the following nouns.

1 3amaarah
2 Taabig
3 issafaarah
4 3iyaadih
5 fawaakih
6 maHal
7 si3ir
8 fikrah

Use five of them in short sentences.

Nominal sentences

Nominal sentences are sentences in which the noun or the pronoun precedes the verb. There are so many sentences that begin with a prepositional phrase or an adverb, but that is an added element. A nominal sentence must have a noun or a pronoun that acts as the subject mostly followed by a verb. The only case in which there is no overt verb in a nominal sentence is the equational sentence. Let's examine the following sentences.

1	**ana kwayyis.**	I am good.
2	**3ammaan madiinih kbiirih.**	Amman is a big town.
3	**ma3i sayyaarah jdiidih.**	I have a new car.
4	**xaalid raaH 3ala issuug.**	Khalid went to the market.
5	**il?awlaad naamu.**	The boys slept.
6	**imbaariH idduktoor 3imil Haadith.**	Yesterday, the doctor had an accident.
7	**daayman uxti btwwSal mit?axxrih.**	My sister always comes late.
8	**thalaath sayyaaraat Sadmat biba3D.**	Three cars crashed into each other.

In 1, 2 and 3, there are no overt verbs. So these are examples of equational sentences. Notice that in 3, the sentence begins with a prepositional phrase. In 4 and 5, the sentences begin with nouns. In 6 and 7, the sentences begin with adverbs, followed by nouns and then verbs. The following rule applies for all nominal sentences: in nominal sentences, the verb must agree in number and gender with the subject. What does this mean? If the subject is singular, the verb must be singular. If the subject is plural, the verb is plural. And in terms of gender, if the subject is feminine, the verb must be feminine. And if it is masculine, the verb is also masculine. Finally, notice the number agreement in sentence 8: the noun is plural non-human and the verb is feminine singular. This is the rule in Arabic for non-human subjects: their agreement pattern is equal to feminine singular.

Exercise 5

Change the following sentences from verbal to nominal sentences.

1 raaHat muna 3ala markiz il?amal.
2 bti3rif muna ishshaari3 kwayyis.
3 ?a3Taani idduktoor dawa mumtaaz.
4 baarak allaah fiik.
5 ?axadna arba3 muHaaDaraat ilyoom.

Verbal sentences

Unlike nominal sentences, verbal sentences are not abundant in LA. However, verbal sentences are very abundant in MSA. Therefore, they can be equally plentiful in academic language, which bridges so many gaps between MSA and the dialects. Verbal sentences are easier in terms of agreement in that they tolerate violations of number agreement when the subject is plural. In other words, if the verb precedes the subject and the subject is plural, the verb can either be plural or singular. Gender agreement, though, continues to hold. The following examples replicate the sentences above but the subject-verb order is reversed. Of course equational sentences are excluded due to the lack of an overt subject.

1 **raaH xaalid 3ala issuug.**	Khalid went to the market.
2 **naam/naamu il?awlaad.**	The boys slept.
3 **imbaariH 3imil idduktoor Haadith.**	Yesterday, the doctor had an accident.
4 **daayman btwwSal uxti mit?axxrih.**	My sister always comes late.
5 **Sadmat thalaath sayyaaraat biba3D.**	Three cars crashed into each other.

Exercise 6

Change the following sentences from nominal to verbal sentences.

1 soofia laazim truuH 3ala il3iyaadih.
2 iTTullaab bidhum yzuuru masjid iljaam3ah.
3 maark ishtara xuDaar min 3ind abu kariim.
4 ana w ukhti binHibb nshuuf aflaam amriikiyyih.
5 leyla bti3raf inha laazim tsaafir bukrah.

Exercise 7

Read the following excerpts. Some verbs, nouns and adjectives do not fit. Find them, cross them out and write the correct answer.

1 ya xaalid, shu fiih 3indik imbaariH?
2 xaalid: ma raH kaan 3ndi shi.
3 intah bukrah bitl3abi kurat qadam?
4 ana mish biddi ʔashtari fawaakih jdiid.
5 biddi ana w iTTullab yruuH 3ala irbid.
6 uxti amiirah ishtari talifoon jdiidih.

Exercise 8 (Bonus audio 34)

If you have the audio, listen to the words and phrases, repeat and write them down.

Unit Eleven

شو مالك؟

shuu maalak?

What's wrong with you?

In this unit, you will learn about:

- Health issues
- Parts of the body
- Precautions
- Quantifiers
- Comparative and superlative forms

Health

Health services are generally available in the Arab world, but they vary from one country to another and from one place to another within the same country. In Jordan, for example, health services are offered by government, military and private providers. Public hospitals and clinics offer health services for all citizens and visitors. They usually require a proof of identity. Military health services are offered to active duty personnel, army veterans and their families. These two types of service are very affordable but usually very crowded. Private health providers are more convenient but significantly more expensive. Table 11.1 presents words commonly used to talk about health. Keep in mind that words that do not have an adjective of the same root as the noun can be used with /**ma3uh . . .** / or /**3induh . . .** /

Table 11.1 Health and medicine (**Audio 2.36**)

LA		English
Noun	*Adjective*	*Noun*
Sudaa3	**mSaddi3**	headache
Haraarah	—	fever
maghiS	**mamghuuS**	stomach ache
dooxah	**daayix**	dizziness
ta3ab	**ta3baan**	tiredness
maraD	**mariiD**	illness
Hasaasiyyih	—	allergy
rashHah	**mrashshiH**	cold
gaHHah	—	cough
ishaal	**mashuul**	diarrhea
imsaak	—	constipation
waja3	—	pain
?alam	—	pain
influwanza	**mfalwiz**	flu

Table 11.2 presents parts of the body.

Table 11.2 Parts of the body (**Audio 2.37**)

LA	English	LA	English
raas (pl. ruus)	head	?iid (pl. ?ideyn)	hand
sha3r/sha3ir	hair	kuu3 (pl. kwaa3)	elbow
idhin (pl. adhaan)	ear	kaff (pl. kfuuf)	palm
thumm/timm	mouth	iSbi3 (pl. aSaabi3)	finger
sinn/snaan	tooth	faxdhih (pl. fxaadh)	hip
munxaar/xashim	nose	rukbah (pl. rukab)	knee
3eyn/3yuun	eye	rijil (ijreyn)	leg
liHyih (pl. illHa)	beard; chin	Sibi3 rijil	toe
ragabah	neck	waSt/xiSir	waist
kitif (pl. ktaaf)	shoulder	DHahir/Dahir	back
Sidir	chest	lsaan	tongue
baTin	belly	DHifir (pl. aDHaafir)	nail
Surrah	belly button	jilid	skin

LA uses cover words or euphemisms to refer to private body parts. These expressions vary by region. Generally, talking about private parts, even using scientific jargon, is frowned upon in Arab culture outside of academic fields. People might use /3iddih/ (lit., tools) to refer to the penis or vagina, /xalfiiyih/ (lit., background) to refer to one's bottom and /Sidir/ (chest) is used to refer to breasts.

 Dialogue 1 (**Audio 2.38**)

 Manar is not feeling well. She does not know exactly what's wrong. Amani is trying to guess.

MANAAR: ana ta3baanih ilyoom.
AMAANI: salaamtik, shuu maalik? bishuu Haassih?
MANAAR: maa ba3rif, raasi biwajji3ni. w kull jismi ta3bann.
AMAANI: 3indik Haraarah?

MANAAR: 3indi Haraarah xafiifih. bass kamaan ma3i maghiS.
AMAANI: mumkin ?akalti shii mish naDiif?
MANAAR: ?akalt shaawirma. w halla? shakli daayxah.
AMAANI: Haraarah, w maghiS, w dooxah, laazim truuHi 3ala
          3iyaadit iljaam3ah.
MANAAR: ma3ik Ha?.
AMAANI: salaamtik.

Vocabulary

ta3baan	tired
Haass	feeling (I'm feeling)
wajji3ni (w+j+3)	to hurt
jisim (pl. ajsaam)	body
xafiif	light; moderate; not severe
maghiS	stomach ache
naDiif	clean
halla?	now
daayix	dizzy
dooxah	dizziness
Ha? (Hag)	right

New expressions

shuu maalik?: lit., what's with you? This question is warranted when
one does not look well.

   Haass Haali: lit., feeling myself. This expression is used to express
how one feels. It is followed either by an adjective or by a verbal
sentence.

> **leyla bitguul inha Haassih Haalha ta3baanih. maa raH tiiji**
> **3al jaam3ah.**
> Laila say she feels (herself to be) tired. She won't come to
> the university.

ma3ik Ha? (or ma3ik Hag): lit., you're right. This expression is used to indicate one is in agreement with a statement made or an opinion given.

> **Lamma gult innuh kadhdhaab, kaan ma3i Hag.**
> When I said he was a liar, I was right.

 Exercise 1

Translate Dialogue 1 above. Avoid using a dictionary.

Expressions using names of parts of the body

Arab culture utilizes plenty of expressions and idioms using names of parts of the body. You have already learned some of them in previous units. Other common expressions are introduced below. Some of these expressions use verbs in the imperative. Some of them keep their meaning with different pronouns while others are fossilized, i.e., they lose their idiomatic meaning once the pronoun is changed. This is the case with so many idiomatic expressions: they do not tolerate changes of their elements. Understanding and using idiomatic expressions is crucial to advancing performance in the language and culture. Literal meaning is provided in brackets.

3ala raasi: (on my head) sure, it's my pleasure. Used in response to a thank-you statement for some service or some favor you are offered.

mish bi?iidi, (mis biidi): (not in my hand) out of my reach, I cannot do it. Used when you want to express inability to offer some service or do a favor because it is beyond your means. The message here is that you're willing to help but you can't. Sometimes, people say "**ilmawduu3 Tili3 min ?iidi**," which means "the favor requested left my hand." This has the same meaning.

> **muS3ab za3laan 3asham maa saa3adtuh. bass ilmawDuu3 mish biiddi.**
> Musab is angry because I did not help him. But the issue is out of my hands.

?adhaanuh Twaal: (his ears are long). Used to say that someone is stupid, not smart. In LA culture, this hints at a similarity to donkeys, whose ears are long. Unfairly, donkeys are symbols of stupidity. The expression is informal and entails much sarcasm.

laa tguul ?adhaanuh Twaal. haadha kalaam mish kwayyis.
Do not say his ears are long. This talk is not good.

sakkir thummak: (shut your mouth). Used to ask someone to shut up. It's a rather impolite expression.

laa tiHki heyk. bass, laa tiHki heyk, xalaS, sakkir thummak!
Don't speak like this. Do not speak like this. That's it, shut your mouth!

bimshi 3ala ruus aSaab3uh: (he's walking on the tips of his toes), expression of pride or great happiness. One who walks on the tips of his toes is either very proud or is in a great state of happiness. Sometimes, people use it to mean that someone is arrogant.

ukhti ishtarat xaatim dhahab ghaali ktiir. halla? btimshi 3ala ruus aSaabi3ha.
My sister bought an expensive gold ring. Now she's walking on the tips of her toes.

3ala munxaari/3ala xashmi: (on my nose), just like *3ala raasi*, above. The only difference is that this is much less likely to be used by women.
   bi3yuuni: (in/with my eyes), just like *3ala raasi*, above. The difference here is that this entails much care about doing something.
   tikram liHyitak: (your beard or chin is honored; honoring your beard). Used to express happiness at doing someone a favor, in response to a thank-you statement. A similar phrase that is commonly used among women is **tikram 3yuunik**.
   ragabati saddaadih: (my neck is covering up). Used to say that I'm ready to cover you up, I have your back covered, or I will deal with all problems.
   Sidruh waasi3: (his chest is wide). Used to express that someone is patient, tolerant and forgiving. The opposite is **Sidruh DHayyig**.

ma3 innak Hakeyt 3annuh kalaam mish kwayyis, Sidruh waasi3 w maa biz3al 3aleyk.
Though you spoke bad words about him, he's forgiving and he won't be angry at you.

Isaanuh Tawiil: (his tongue is long), talkative in a bad way, not polite.

haadha ilustaadh Isaanuh Tawiil, maa biHtarim iTTullaab.
This teacher's tongue is long. He does not respect students.

baTnuh kbiir: (his belly is big). Used to express that someone is gluttonous, greedy, piggish. It could mean that someone loves food a lot, but the term is derogatory.

SaaHib iddukkaan baTnuh kbiir, biHibb ilmaSaari kthiir.
The shop's owner is greedy. He loves money so much.

sinnuh Tayyib: (his tooth is OK). Used to say that someone has a very good appetite. Mostly this is kind expression.

SaaHbi aHmad sinnuh Tayyib, biHibb ilmasahaawi akthar min ummuh.
My friend's appetite is big. He loves grilled food more than his mother.

jilid txiin or samiik: (his skin is thick). Used to express that someone is resistant to blame or does not care about people's criticism. Sometimes, it could refer to someone who tolerates much kidding and joking at his expense and does not get mad easily.

dammuh thagiil: (his blood is thick). Used to refer to someone not pleasant to be around, description of bad company. The opposite is **dammuh xafiif**.

Exercise 2

Read the names of the following public figures. Use an expression to address them. You can choose to describe them, give them a compliment, talk about their behavior, etc. See the example.

Example: Nelson Mandela: **intih 3ala raasi.**
Paris Hilton: **leysh inti daayman btimshi 3ala ruus aSaab3ik?**

1 George Bush
2 Bill Cosby
3 Rush Limbaugh
4 Jennifer Aniston
5 Bill Gates
6 Oprah Winfrey

Cultural point

Precautions

Apart from precautions related to personal security, health risks might also be a source of discomfort. Despite some general stereotypes, the major sources of health problems usually have to do with personal choices in terms of food and drink. While most foods are clean, getting sick or catching some kind of food parasite remains almost inevitable. Visitors to the Middle East often report catching parasites after consuming fruits, vegetables or undercooked foods. Water is also a possible source. Symptoms are usually limited to stomach ache, headache, dizziness, vomiting and diarrhea. Patients usually recover quickly.

Trips and excursions are also occasions for getting sick. Some people like to sample different, sometimes exotic types of food during their trips, which can cause health problems. Heat is another reason especially during the summer or in the desert where the temperature is hot during the day and cold and breezy at night. Here are some tips:

- Drink bottled water. Most Arabs avoid drinking tap water, despite its relative safety. The reason is that water resources are scarce, especially in the Levant and therefore several elements are used in water treatment.
- Avoid eating raw foods, especially raw meat. Most Arabs cook their food well, though.
- Limit eating fresh fruits and vegetables to one item at a time. This is a good way of eliminating foods that can cause health problems.
- If you buy your own food, stick to clean providers.
- Avoid buying foods from street vendors. Most of the time, cleanliness is at low levels here.
- Drink a lot of water, especially on hot days. Dehydration is likely due to hot and dry weather.
- If you are on any kind of medication, bring it with you.
- Long sleeves are advisable. They help you avoid sunburn.

Exercise 3

You're getting ready to go on a weekend trip. Your host mother is worried and wants to make sure you are taking enough precautions. Tell her five things you did to get ready. See the example:

Example: ana ma3i talifoon. law Saar fiih mushkilih,
baHki ma3ik.

Dialogue 2 (Audio 2.39–2.40)

Elizabeth and Nicole are on a trip to the Jordanian desert. Elizabeth is not feeling well. Nicole asks for help from their teacher, Omar.

ILIZABITH:	3indi ?alam shadiid fi baTani.
NICOLE:	maghiS? salaamtik.
ILIZABITH:	shikluh maghiS.
NICOLE:	?akiid ?akalti shi ghalaT.
ILIZABITH:	maa ?akalt ay shi jdiid. salaTah w xubiz w ruzz.
NICOLE:	yimkin min issalaTah.
ILIZABITH:	aah, laazim ?aruuH 3alHammaam bsur3ah.

Elizabeth leaves and then comes back.

NICOLE:	halla? aHsan?
ILIZABITH:	ya3ni, bass lissa ilmaghiS maa raaH.
NICOLE:	xalliini aHki lal ustaadh 3umar.
NICOLE:	ustaadh 3umar, ilizabith ta3baanih w 3indha maghiS.
3UMAR:	salamtik ya ilizabith.
ILIZABITH:	allaah ysallmak, fiih ay duktoor hoon?
3UMAR:	maa biddik duktoor. hassa bni3mallik kaasit meyrameyyih.
ILIZABITH:	bass ana mariiDah.
3UMAR:	kaasit meyrameyyih w bitSiiri tamaam.

Vocabulary

shadiid	strong, severe
ghalaT	wrong
ruzz	rice
Hammaam (pl. Hammamaat)	bathroom
ya3ni	almost
xalli (x+l+l+y)	to let
meyrameyyih	sage
bitSiiri (S+y+r)	to become

Exercise 4

Use each of the following in a sentence:

1 shadiid
2 ghalaT
3 ya3ni
4 xalli
5 (S+y+r)

Exercise 5

Samira is suffering from a terrible stomach ache. She has kept a log of her illness on cards but the cards are mixed up. Rearrange them and write a short report using her notes in order. Feel free to use connectors or add words as needed. Be brief and concise.

1 ?alam baSiit fi baTni.
2 ?akalt shwayyit salaTah ma3 ruzz w jaaj.
3 waja3 shadiid fi baTni.
4 Hakeyt ma3 SaHibti.
5 Saar 3indi ishaal ma3 dooxah.
6 SaHibti gaalat ishrabi za3tar (zaatar).
7 shribit 3aSiir.
8 nimit w lissa baTni biwajji3ni.

Quantifiers: kull, ba3D, shwayyih, nidfih, wala
كل، بعض، شوية، ندفة، ولا

> **kull:** all, every
> **ba3D**, or **ba3DH:** some of
> **shwayyih:** little of, few of
> **nidfih:** few of
> **wala:** none of

These particles precede nouns. When using these quantifiers, LA makes no distinction between countable or uncountable nouns. The meanings of these quantifiers are close to their translations. *shwayyih* indicates a little more than *nidfih* does. Whether the noun after these particles is definite or indefinite depends on contextual factors. Let's consider the following examples; an asterisk indicates wrong usage.

1	**kull innaas**	all of the people
2	*****kull naas**	*all people
3	**kull waaHad**	everyone
4	**kulhum**	all of them
5	**ba3D innaas**	some of the people
6	**ba3D naas**	some people
7	**ba3Dhum**	some of them
8	**shwayyit ruzz**	some rice
9	**shwayyit noom**	some sleep
10	**shwayyit naas**	a few people
11	*****shwayyithum**	*a few of them
12	**nidfit miliH**	little salt
13	*****nidfit naas**	*few people
14	*****nidfithum**	*few of them
15	**wala waaHad**	not anyone
16	*****wala naas**	*not any people
17	*****walahum**	*not any of them

Exercise 6

Answer each of the following questions; use quantifiers.

1 umm aHmad bidha _____ min iddukkaan?
2 il?akil zaaki (delicious) bass bidduh _____ miliH.
3 ishshaari3 _____ sayyaaraat. raH nitaxxar 3an ilbeyt.
4 kaan iljaw kthiir baarid, _____ min ilbeyt.
5 _____ innaas biHibbu ilfalaafil, w _____ biHibbu
  ilmashaawi.

Comparative and superlative forms

LA uses one simple form to express comparative and superlative adjectives. For the former, the comparison is held between two identical entities, where one has more of the "adjective" than the other. For superlative adjectives, LA uses a comparative form followed by a noun that refers to the whole category. Table 11.3 presents comparative and superlative adjectives.

Table 11.3 Comparative and superlative forms
(Audio 2.41; Bonus audio 36)

Adjective	Comparative	Superlative	English
kthiir	akthar min	akthar shi waaHad	plentiful
galiil	agall min	agall shi/waaHad	little; few
kabiir	akbar min	akbar shi/waaHad	big
Saghiir	aSghar min	aSghar shi/waaHad	small
Tawiil	aTwal min	aTwal waaHad/shi	long/tall
dhaki	adhka min	adhka waaHad	smart
Hilu	aHla min	aHla shi/waaHad	pretty; beautiful
gawi	agwa min	agwa waaHad	strong
Sa3b	aS3ab min	aS3ab shi/waaHad	difficult
sahil	ashal min	ashal waaHad/shi	easy

Notice that comparative adjectives are followed by /**min**/ to compare two identical entities, but that the superlative form is followed by a noun that refers to the whole category. Consider the following examples:

1 **Irbid akbar min izzarga.**
   Irbid is bigger than Zarqa.
2 **3ammaan akbar madiinih fi ilurdun.**
   Amman is the biggest city in Jordan.
3 **leyla aHla min saamya.**
   Laila is more beautiful than Samia.
4 **ilbatra aHla makaan fi ila3aalam.**
   Petra is the most beautiful place in the world.
5 **haadha iddars aS3ab dars fi il3arabi.**
   This lesson is the most difficult lesson in Arabic.
6 **mannar adhka bint fi iSSaff.**
   Manar is the smartest girl in the class.
7 **?ibni agwa walad fi ilmadrasih.**
   My son is the strongest boy in school.
8 **liina aHla min kull SaaHbaatha.**
   Leena is more beautiful than all of her friends.
9 **si3ir libyuut fi 3ammaam agall min si3rha fi il3afgabih.**
   The price of homes in Amman is less than the price in Aqaba.
10 **axuuy aSghar min ukhti.**
   My brother is younger/smaller than my sister.

 ## Exercise 7

Decide whether you need to use comparative or superlative adjectives
in each of the following.

1 madiinit dimashq _____ madiinit 3amman. (kabiirih)
2 xaali saalim _____ waaHad bikull axwaali. (kabiir)
3 mumkin ykuun Bill Gates _____ insaan fi il3aalam. (dhaki)
4 ana biHibb ishshay _____ ilgahwah. (kthiir)
5 maark _____ Taalib fi iSSaff, 3umruh 3ishriin sanih. (Saghiir)
6 _____ mushkilih kaanat lamma saafarit 3ala ilyaman. (Sa3b)

Exercise 8

Use a comparative or a superlative adjective for each of the following.

> **Example:** jaam3at dimashq iljaam3ah ilurduniiyih.
> **jaam3at dimashq agdam min iljaam3ah ilurduniiyih.**
> Damascus University is older than Jordan University.

1 sayyaraat Toyota _____ sayyaraat niisaan. (gawi: strong)
2 burj eiffil fi faransa _____ shi fi baariis. (Hilu)
3 issamak _____ iljaaj fi ilurdun. (ghaali: expensive)
4 il3agabih _____ madiinih 3an 3amman. (ba3iid)
5 ilbaaS _____ issayyaarah bikthiir. (Tawiil)

Exercise 9 (Bonus audio 37)

If you have the audio, listen to the words and phrases, repeat and write them down.

Unit Twelve

الجو

iljaw

The weather

In this unit, you will learn about:

- Weather
- Seasons of the year
- Broken plurals
- **gabil wa ba3d + ma**

Weather

The Middle East enjoys different climates. Even within a small country the size of Jordan, temperatures can range from a high of 85°F to 105°F (30°C to 40°C). During summer, for example, northern parts of Jordan are mild to hot during the day but mostly breezy and moderate at night, whereas it can be really hot in the Jordan Valley, Aqaba, the Dead Sea and the desert areas. In winter, the northern part of the country gets much more rainfall and snow compared to the desert areas. Table 12.1 presents new vocabulary that is associated with weather.

Table 12.1 Weather vocabulary **(Audio 2.42)**

LA	English	LA	English
Haalit iTTags	weather forecast	**nashrah jawwiiyih**	weather forecast
iljaw	the weather	**gamar**	moon
mu3tadil	mild	**shams**	sun
Haami/shoob/Harr	hot	**hawa**	wind, air
naar	blazing (lit. fire)	**riiH**	storm; strong wind
baarid/sag3ah/ msaggi3	cold	**ghabarah**	dust
riTib	humid	**mghabbir**	dusty
maTar	rain	**Hawarah**	ice; sleet
btishti/bitmaTTir	it's raining	**sama?**	sky
thalij	snow	**nijmih (pl. njuum)**	star
btithlij	it's snowing	**gheymih (pl. ghyuum)**	cloud
fayaDHaan	flooding	**ra3id**	thunder
mghayyim	cloudy	**DHabaab**	fog
barg	lightning	**qaws quzaH**	rainbow

Dialogue 1 (Audio 2.43–2.44)

Mark and Abdallah are planning a weekend trip. They're discussing the weather forecast.

MAARK: keyf raayiH ykuun iljaw fi ilbatra nihaayit il?usboo3?
3ABDALLAH: fi ilbatra raH yikuun iljaw Haami, bass mish kthiir.

MAARK: ya3ni bikuun kwayyis?
3ABDALLAH: in shaa allaah. darajit ilHaraarah Hawaali iththneyn w
              thalaathiin.
MAARK: Haami shway bass mish baTTaal.
3ABDALLAH: laakin il3agabah raH tkuun naar.
MAARK: kam raH tkuun?
3ABDALLAH: innashrah il jawwiiyih bitguul waaHad w arb3iin.
MAARK: yaa laTiif! fi3lan naar.
3ABDALLAH: shuu ra?yak nruuH 3ala 3ajloon aHsan?
MAARK: xalliini ?afakkir bilmawDuu3.

Vocabulary

nihaayih (pl. nihaayaat)	end
?usboo3 (pl. asaabii3)	week
ya3ni	so
darajih (pl. darajaat)	step; degree
fi3lan	truly, for sure
?afakkir (f+k+k+r)	to think
mawDuu3 (pl. mawaaDii3)	topic, subject, issue

New expressions

mish baTTaal: not bad. This expression is used to describe something
as being OK.

   yaa laTiif!: an expression of exclamation. **laTiif** is one of Allah's
names. In Muslim culture, Allah has 100 names, each signifying
one of His traits. For example, **raHmaan:** merciful; **laTiif:** kind;
qaadir: capable; **3aaTi:** giver, etc. Arabs and Muslims use these
names after **yaa** (a particle for calling on someone) when they ask
for Allah's help.

Seasons of the year

As you will see, in the Arab world there are several holidays, foods or festivities that are associated with different seasons. The types of food available, especially in the Levant, are not the same during all seasons. Social demographics sometimes change in different seasons. As strange as this sounds, it is normal when you think of the hundreds of thousands of Arabs who live outside of their countries and decide to spend their vacations at home. Some towns in Jordan increase their population by nearly a quarter during summer time. Table 12.2 below introduces vocabulary associated with seasons of the year.

Table 12.2 Seasons of the year and related vocabulary **(Audio 2.45)**

LA	English	LA	English
faSil (pl. fuSuul)	season	**3azuumah**	invitation
Seyf	summer	**dafa?**	warmth
shita/shatwiiyih	winter	**warid**	flowers
rabii3	spring	**fattaH (ilwarid)**	to blossom (of flowers)
xariif	fall	**dhibil**	to wither
?ija (+ season)	to come	**3ushub**	grass
muntazah	park	**Hashiish**	grass
sahrah	night get-together	**riiHah/3uTur**	fragrance

Exercise 1

Group the following words so that they fit the category of each group below. A given word might fall in more than one group.

mu3tadil	Haami	shoob	Harr	naar	baarid
sag3ah	msaggi3	riTib	maTar	thalij	fayaDHaan
barg	gamar	shams	hawa	riiH	ghabarah
Hawarah	sama?	njuum	ghyuum	ra3id	qaws quzaH

Seyf
xariif
shita
rabii3

Exercise 2

Using words and expressions from this and previous units, write what you do in each of the following seasons. See the example:

Example: shu bti3mal fi iSSeyf?
           fi iSSeyf basbaH, bal3ab kurat qadam, baruuH
           riHlaat, w bass-har kthiir.
           In summer, I swim, play soccer, go on trips and stay
           up late.

1 shuu bit3mali fi irrabii3?
2 shuu bti3imal fi ishshita?
3 shuu bti3mal fi ilxariif?

Dialogue 2 **(Audio 2.46–2.47)**

Tom is asking Murad about the different activities during the different seasons of the year.

TOOM: ya muraad, bti3rif shuu fiih nashaaTaat fi ilurdun biSSeyf?
MURAAD: Tab3an. shahr sittih mumtaaz la irriHlaat, mashaawi
         a shammaat hawa.
TOOM: Tayyib. shahir sab3ah Haami kthiir.
MURAAD: SaHiiH. 3indak mahrajaan jarash. akthar nashaaTaatuh
         billeyl.
TOOM: ana baHib ilmahrajaanaat. Intih shuu bti3mal fi ishshita?
MURAAD: 3alashaan iljaw bikuun bard, ana baruuH 3ala il3agabih.
TOOM: jawwha bikuun mu3tadil bishshita??
MURAAD: ?akiid.
TOOM: shuu aHsan faSil 3indak?
MURAAD: aHsan faSil 3indi irrabii3. iljaw bikuun mumtaaz, maa fiih
         zaHmih mithil iSSeyf wala bard mithil ishshita, wala
         ghabarah mithil irrabii3. yaa reyt kull issanih rabii3.
TOOM: yaa salaam. ana akthar faSil baHibbuh iSSeyf.
MURAAD: intu fi bariTaanya shab3aaniin 3ushub w rabii3.

Vocabulary

nashaaT (pl. nashaaTaat)	activity
Tab3an	of course
mahrajaan	festival
leyl	night time
zaHmih	crowded
bariTaanya	Britain
shab3aan	full of; has plenty of

New expressions

shammit hawa: lit., smelling of air. A trip, usually to an open park.

　yaa reyt: I wish. An expression used to express deep longing for something or real need of something. It is usually followed by a sentence rather than a noun phrase.

　yaa salaam: oh, wow. An expression of great admiration or happiness at something.

Exercise 3

Fill in the blanks with the correct word.

mu3atadil	Haami	shoob	Harr	naar	baarid
sag3ah	msaggi3	riTib	maTar	thalij	fayaDHaan
barg	gamar	shams	hawa	riiH	ghabarah
Hawarah	sama?	njuum	ghyuum	ra3id	qaws quzaH

1　il?akil lissa _____ kthiir. mish 3aarif aakul.
2　lamma yikuun iljaw _____ baHibb anaam fi innhaar wa asharr billeyl.
3　fiih _____ w _____ kthiir ilyoom. shikilha raH tmaTTir.
4　lamma tkuun issama zarga, bitkuun il _____ Hilwah kthiir.
5　innaas fi ilurdun biHibbu il _____ kthiir. mish mithil ilamriikaan.

6 swaagit issayyraat sa3bih lamma ykuun fiih _____.

7 iljaw _____ fi ilmasa.

8 kull sanih bikuun fiih _____ fi amriika.

9 ana baHibb ?aruuH riHlaat bass lamma ykuun iljaw _____.

10 fiih _____ galiilih. yimkin maa fiih maTar ilyoom.

Exercise 4

Pick up five new words that you learned about weather in this unit. Use each one of them in a short sentence.

Broken plurals

We have learned the regular plural suffixes for masculine and feminine nouns. But you might also have noticed that irregular plurals, especially for masculine nouns, are plentiful. Broken plurals fall into categories and have rules that we can learn. These categories are based on the consonant-vowel structures of the singular nouns. Therefore, presenting these rules at this stage requires a deeper discussion of word structure and syllabification, a topic usually discussed in linguistics research.[1] One rule that should by now be clear is that the plural form for most feminine singular nouns ending in /**at**/ or /**it**/ is /**-aat**/. This also applies to the majority of non-human singular nouns. Among the best ways to learn forms of broken plurals is to try to find out the plural for every noun you learn.

1 If you are interested, check out Robert Ratcliffe's *The Broken Plural in Arabic and Comparative Semitic*, John Benjamins, 1998.

Exercise 5

Provide the meanings of each of the following nouns, then write the plural forms.

1 aaniseh

2 shabb

3 madiinih

4 Saff

5 maktab

6 diinaar

7 dagiigah

8 shaggah

9 kaasih

10 3inwaan

Use five of them in sentences.

gabil w ba3d + ma

/**gabil**/ and /**ba3d**/ are adverbs of time and place. Consider the following examples:

1 **ilbeyt illi gabil beytna.** The house before our house.
2 **waggif sayyaartak ba3d** Stop your car after the sign.
  ilishaarah.
3 **laa tishrab gahwah gabl innoom.** Don't drink coffee before sleeping.
4 **bukrah ba3d issaa3ah sab3ah.** Tomorrow after 7:00.
5 **raH ashtaghil ba3d ittaxxaruj.** I will work after graduation.
6 **ana bashrab shay gabil innoom.** I drink tea before sleeping.

Notice that these two words are followed by noun phrases, not by sentences. Notice also that sentences 5 and 6 do not have a clear adverb of time or place. However, the sentence structure suggests that one action is related in time to another: in 5, the sentence says the speaker will work after he/she graduates. And in 6, the speaker says he/she drinks tea before going to bed. Both actions in each sentence are clearly sequenced. But the use of /**ma**/ or /**maa**/ with these expressions requires using a sentence. Consider the following examples:

1 **ba3d maa tirja3 min iljaam3ah, ruuH 3ala issuug.**
  After you come back from the university, go to the souk.
2 **gabil maa tnaam, laazim tiHki ma3 ummak.**
  Before you go to bed, you must call your mother.
3 **laa tiHki ma3uh gabil maa yi3tadhir.**
  Don't talk to him before he apologizes.
4 **maa raH ashuufha ba3d ma tsaafir.**
  I won't see her after he leaves (travels).

Exercise 6

Think of your day-to-day activities. Write five sentences in which you mention what you do before or after what. Read the example first.

Example: ana bafTir ba3d ma ashrab gahwah.
             I eat breakfast after I drink tea. (after drinking tea).

Exercise 7

Each of the following sentences has an error in plural forms. Find the errors and rewrite the sentence correctly. Then translate each one of them.

1 ilʔustaadh saʔalni 3an akbar thalaath binaayiin fi 3amman.
2 ghurfit iSSaff kbiirih. Tuulha sabi3 mitraat.
3 mumkin atxarraj ba3d thalaath sanaayin.
4 fiih fi aljaam3ah 3adad kabiir min ilaʔjnabiyyiin.
5 kull yoom 3indi wajibiin. ana t3ibit.
6 fiih guddam iljaam3ah tisi3 baaSiin.
7 ana ba3rif thalaath aw arba3 makaanaat fiiha maTaa3im
   mumtaazih.
8 ishtareyt sitt kursiyaat li ilmaTbax 3indi fil ilbeyt.
9 ummi bidha kamaan thalaath aw arba3 xaatmiin.
10 ukhti bitHibb illoonaat ilʔaHmar w ilʔaswad.

Exercise 8 (Bonus audio 40)

If you have the audio, listen to the words and phrases, repeat and write them down.

Unit Thirteen

كرة القدم

kurat ilqadam

Football (soccer)

In this unit, you will learn about:

- Sports
- **Haki shabaab** (youth talk)
- **kaan**
- **biddi**, **laazim**

Sports

Soccer is by and large the most popular game in the Arab world. Therefore, it occupies much of people's time, especially college-age students, although more so male than female. An increasing number of young Arab men are becoming active fans of certain international soccer teams. Cafés tend to fill up with fans when there are scheduled matches. Fans are also divided when it comes to local soccer teams. Most people tend to support their local teams – those that represent their hometown. Supporting a certain team can sometimes hide some type of political message. Generally, in Jordan fans are divided between two teams where one team represents Jordanians, and the other represents Jordanians of Palestinian origin. While this classification is not 100 per cent accurate, any follower of the demographics of soccer teams' fans can find a pattern along these lines. Sometimes, people watching a game between these two teams use racial and ethnic slurs to express their hatred of the other team. Table 13.1 presents some vocabulary used in sports.

Table 13.1 Sports vocabulary

LA	English	LA	English
fariig (pl. firag)	team	shajja3 (sh+j+3)	to support
laa3ib (laa3ibiin)	player	mubaaraah	match
mudarrib	coach	hujuum	attack
Hakam	referee	difaa3	defense
Haaris marma	goalkeeper	indhaar	warning
jumhuur	audience	tasallul	offside
shaat (sh+w+t)	to shoot (the ball)	iSaabah	injury
marrar (m+r+r)	to pass (the ball)	kurah (pl. kuraat)	ball
faaz (f+w+z)	to win	gool	goal
xisir (x+s+r)	to lose	kaas	cup
sajjal (s+j+l)	to score	mal3ab (pl. malaa3ib)	playground; field
da3am (d+3+m)	to support	najim	star (star player)

Dialogue 1 (Audio 2.48–2.49)

Kamal is at the café watching a football game with George.

JOORJ:	3ala shuu btitfarraj, ya kamaal?
KAMAAL:	intah mish 3aarif? haay mubaaraat riyal madriid w barshaloonah.
JOORJ:	w intah miin bitshajji3?
KAMAAL:	Tab3an barshaloonah. riyal madriid fariig Ta3baan.
JOORJ:	shuu ya3ni law xisir barshaloonah?
KAMAAL:	shuu yixsar barshaloonah? intih majnuun?
JOORJ:	mish gaSdi, bass mumkin yixsaru.
KAMAAL:	mish mumkin, illa idha kaan ilHakam DHiddhum.
JOORJ:	ya3ni ilHakam 3induh mashaakil?
KAMAAL:	daayman ilHukaam bil3abu ma3 riyal madriid.
JOORJ:	w intah leysh mihtamm bi mubaaraah ?uroobiyyih? xalliik bi ilfirag il3arabiyyih.
KAMAAL:	shuu firag 3arabiyyih? maa bi3rafu yil3abu, li3ib Haaraat.
JOORJ:	bass fiih munhum kwaysiin.
KAMAAL:	bala kwaysiin bala baTTiix.

Vocabulary (Audio 2.50)

titfarraj (f+r+r+j)	to watch
riyal madriid	Real Madrid (football team)
barshaloonah	Barcelona (football team)
majnuun	crazy; out of your mind
DHidd	against
mihtamm	interested
?uroobiyyih	European
Haarah (pl. Haaraat)	neighborhood; quarter

New expressions

shuu ya3ni law xisir?: so what if it loses? Used to express indifference.

> **shuu ya3ni law saafarat Habiibti? mish mushkilih.**
> So what if my darling left? It's not a problem.

shuu yixsar barshaloonah?: shuu + verbal sentence. If the tone is similar to the tag question in English, this indicates a strong level of disapproval.

> **shuu tsaafir laHaalha? ?abadan, mish munkin.**
> What, she will travel alone? No way, impossible.

intih majnuun?: are you crazy? A very strong statement of disapproval.

> **tsaafir laHaalha? intih majnuun?**
> She will travel alone? Are you crazy?

mish gaSdi: I did not mean it. A polite apologetic expression.

> **mish gaSdi tsaafir laHalha, ?akiid intih bitsaafir ma3aaha.**
> I did not mean she will travel alone. For sure you will travel with her.

bala + (adj. or noun) bala baTTiix: lit., without (adj. or noun) without watermelons. This is a common expression of neglect of the entity or attribute expressed in the adjective or noun used. The expression in the dialogue above means that the speaker has no appreciation for the assumption that these teams are good.

> **bala asaafir ma3ha bala baTTiix. ana maa baHibb inniswaan.**
> I do not want to travel with her. I do not like women.

Exercise 1

Rearrange the following words in four groups by the heading provided. Some words might fall under more than one heading. Be prepared to discuss your answer.

Haaris marma	shaat	marrar	faaz	xisir
sajjal	da3am	shajja3	mubaaraah	hujuum
difaa3	indhaar	tasallul	iSaabah	kurah
gool	kaas	mal3ab	najim	

fariig
laa3ib
muddarib
jumhuur

Exercise 2

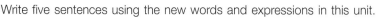

Write five sentences using the new words and expressions in this unit.

Dialogue 2 (Audio 2.51–2.52)

Amjad is sad that his favorite team lost a football match. He's
talking to his sister, Nawal, about the match.

NAWAAL:	shuu maalak, ya amjad? leysh za3laan?
AMJAD:	aax ya nawaal, ilyoom xsirna ahamm mubaaraah fi ilmawsim.
NAWAAL:	mubaaraat shuu?
AMJAD:	kaas ilurdun, ilfeySali xisir thaalaath waaHad laSaaliH ilwiHdaat.
NAWAAL:	basiiTah. in shaa allaah ilmarrah iththaanyih bifuuzu.
AMJAD:	shuu marrah thaanyih? haay ilmubaaraah innihaaʔiyyih.
NAWAAL:	ana mish 3aarfih leysh intah za3laan ktiir.
AMJAD:	bagullik xsirna ilmubaaraah innihaaʔiyyih.
NAWAAL:	ya axi, xsirna falasTiin w li3raag w suuriyya, w liibya w intih za3laan 3ala mubaaraah?
AMJAD:	shuu daxxal irriyaaDHah bissiyaasih?
NAWAAL:	keyf shuu daxxallhum?
AMJAD:	ana leysh baHki ma3ik min ilʔasaas?

Vocabulary

za3laan	mad; angry
aax!	ouch!; alas
mawsim (pl. mawaasim)	season
ilfeySali	Al-Faisali, Jordanian soccer team
thaalaath waaHad	three to one
SaaliH	in favor of; for
ilwiHdaat	Al-Wihdat, Jordanian soccer team
basiiTah	easy; not a problem
marrah (pl. marraat)	one time; once
nihaaʔi	final
agullik (g+w+l)	to say
daxal (d+x+l)	to enter
ʔasaas	basis

New expressions

ana mish 3aarfih leysh: I do not know why. Used when one does not have an explanation for something, or for doing something.

shuu daxxal irriyaaDHah bissiyaasih: what does sports have to do with politics! (**shuu daxxal A bi B?**). An expression used to express that two things are not related.

ana leysh baHki ma3ik min ilʔasaas?: why am I talking to you in principle (**leysh** someone does something **min ilʔasaas!**)? This expression is to indicate that discussion of a given issue or doing something is fruitless, in vain.

Exercise 3

Derive as many words as you can from each of the following. Then use one form of each word in a sentence. See the example:

Example: daxal: daxxal, daxal, daxxalni, daxlih, ma daxalni, ma daxalish.

1 tfarraj
2 za3laan
3 marrah
4 aguul
5 ʔasaas

Cultural point

Haki shabaab

One might wonder what issues young people in the Arab world talk about. And the fact of the matter is that there is virtually no way one can a find a suitable answer to this question. Issues that attract people's attention in the Arab world are not much different from other places around the world. There is, however, a greater interest in politics, religion and issues of conflict in comparison to, say, an average American or European. This is a trend motivated by the general belief that the political situation in the region, over which people of the region have very little control, affects people's livelihood. Young people, university students in particular, are usually worried about their lives beyond graduation. But issues related to the opposite sex are also very prevalent due, in part, to the greater distance between the two sexes compared to non-Muslim countries.

Women are also becoming increasingly worried about their opportunities in the workforce. As economies of the Levant plunge, women are increasingly looking for jobs in areas they have not traditionally tried before.

Dialogue 3 (Audio 2.53–2.54)

Listen to the following phone call from a young Jordanian man, Isamael, to a popular radio program, *With the People*.

ISMAA3IIN[1]: aluu, aluu, marHabba 3ammi.
RADIO HOST: ahleyn axi, itfaDDal, intih 3al hawa. miin ma3i?
ISMAA3IIN: ana 3al hawa? yi3Tiik il3aafyih ustaadh saalim.

RADIO HOST: allaah y3aafiik. itfaDDal axi, shuu mushkiltak?

ISMAA3IIN: mushkilti inni mish 3al hawa, mushkilti inni maakil hawa.

RADIO HOST: balaash niHki heyk, ya axi. shuu mushikltak, law samHaht?

ISMAA3IIN: ana Saar li sabi3 saniin mitxarrij min iljaam3ah w maa 3indi shughul.

RADIO HOST: sabi3 saniin? shuu taxaSSuSak?

ISMAA3IIN: taxaSSuSi 3uluum siyaasiyyih.

RADIO HOST: Tayyib ya axi, ?istanna shway, sanih aw santeyn.

ISMAA3IIN: ?istanneyt sabi3 saniin, bala faaydih. shuu a3mal, fiih naas txarraju ba3di w ishtaghalu. bass la?innuh ana maa 3indi waasTah, maa illi shughul.

RADIO HOST: maa fiih waasTah yaa axi. ?istanna doorak w kull shi bikuun tamaam. bnaaxudh ittiSaal thaani, aluu!

1 Most Jordanians write this name as اسماعيل and pronounce it as اسماعين.

Vocabulary

balaash (+verb)	there is no need to
Saar li	it has been (time)
shughul	job
3ilm (pl. 3uluum)	science
siyaasih (pl. syaasaat)	politics; policy
?istanna (?+s+t+n+y)	to wait
faaydih (pl. fawaa?id)	profit, benefit
ishtaghalu (sh+gh+l)	to work
waasTah (pl. waasTaat)	mediation; middleman
door (pl. ?adwaar)	line; turn
naaxudh (?+x+dh)	to take
ittiSaal (pl. ittiSaalaat)	call; phone call

New expressions

3al hawa: on air, live. Using this expression is only restricted to TV or radio shows

    (allaah) yi3Tiik il3aafyih: may (Allah) give you wellness. This expression is sometimes used as a greeting. It can also be used to express thanks to someone for doing something.

    allaah y3aafiik: may Allah keep/protect you. This is the answer to the previous greeting.

    maakil hawa: lit., I'm eating air/wind. This is a slang expression meaning one is in a desperate situation, or one is too tired.

    bala faaydih: without benefit. This expression means "in vain."

Exercise 4

Read Dialogue 2 again. Summarize the caller's complaint in writing.

kaan

This verb is the Arabic version of the verb "to be" in English. Before presenting the different usages of this verb in LA, it's important to remember the difference between two grammatical forms: (-ing forms such as playing, eating, etc.) and (-ed forms such as played, eaten). LA expresses these two functions using a /**kaan**/ verb along with the main verb in two derivations: subject noun and object noun. The subject noun is used to express the doer of the verb. The object noun is used to express who was affected by the action of the verb, i.e. the receiver of the action in the verb. Without the presence of a full verb along with /**kaan**/, there will be an equational sentence in a form other than the present tense. Consider the following examples:

1 **kunt ta3baan.**
    I was tired.
2 **kaanat Hilwah lamma kaanat Sghiirih.**
    She was pretty when she was young.
3 **kunna msaafriin.**
    We were traveling.

4 **kaanu shabaab muHtaramiin.**
   They were respected young men.
5 **kaan ma3i ktaab.**
   I had (with me) a book.
6 **kaan 3indha mushkilih.**
   She had (with her) a problem.
7 **kunt bal3ab kurat qadam zamaan.**
   I was playing soccer (in the past).
   I used to play soccer (in the past).
8 **salma kaanat tidrus biljaam3ah.**
   Salma was studying at the university.
   Salma used to study at the university.

Notice the following: in 1–3, the structure in Arabic is the verb, which has a subject pronoun (I, she, we, respectively) followed by the remainder of the sentence. This is an equational sentence. In 4, the subject is a pronounced noun, not a pronoun. In 5 and 6, there is a prepositional phrase after /**kaan**/. In 7 and 8, there is a full verb following the verb /**kaan**/. This is how Arabic expresses an action that took place over time in the past but is now completed.

 ## Exercise 5

Translate each of the following sentences using /**kaan**/.

1 My brother used to play football when he was young.
2 The food at the restaurant was the best I ever had in my life.
3 We were watching a football match when the teacher entered class.
4 I had a very nice car when I was in Japan.
5 My friends were not going to travel to Europe.

biddi, laazim

We have seen these two words several times in the previous units. Both are used to express the need to have something or to do something. Consider the following examples; sentences marked with an asterisk are grammatically incorrect.

1 I need a new car
  biddi sayyaarah jdiidih.
  laazimni sayyaarah jdiidih.
  ***laazim sayyaarah jdiidih.**
2 I want to travel to China
  biddi asaafir 3ala iSSiin.
  laazim asaafir 3ala iSSiin.
  ***laazimni asaafir 3ala iSSiin.**

The main difference between /**biddi**/ and /**laazim**/ is the fact that the former already entails a subject (I, in this case) but the second one does not. Therefore, in the absence of a clear subject, /**laazim**/ cannot be used. And when the sentence has a subject, adding a subject pronoun to /**laazim**/ causes redundancy.

Exercise 6

The following sentences have some errors. Find the errors and correct the sentences.

1 ana baddhum yil3ab kurat qadam issaa3ah arba3ah masaa.
2 laazimhum adrus kull yoom thaman saa3aat Hatta anjaH.
3 xaalid bidha yishtari HummuS w falaafil.
4 ana w samiira laazimhin nruuH 3ala ilmaT3am.
5 uxti bidhum kamaan arba3 shaalaat.

Conditional statement: laʔin, 3alashaan . . . laazim, bass

Conditional statements behave very much like cause and effect statements. The same particles can be used in either type of the sentences. Study the following sentences:

1 **laʔinnuh ana maa 3indi waasTah, maa illi shughul.**
  Because I do not have a middleman, I do not have a job.
2 **3alashaan tinjaH, laazim tidrus.**
  So that you can pass, you have to study.
3 **bass tiSall ilbeyt, ittaSil ma3i.**
  When you arrive home, call me.

You can switch the order of the two phrases within each of the sentences above without causing any difference in meaning. No subject-verb inversion is required. The only difference is that the new structure does not require the use of a comma in writing.

1 maa illi shughul laʔinnuh ana maa 3indi waasTah.
2 laazim tidrus 3alashaan tinjaH.
3 ittaSil ma3i bass tiSal ilbeyt.

Exercise 7

Complete each of the following sentences.

1 ustaadhna za3laan laʔinnuh
2 ustaadhna za3laan laʔinnana
3 bass tshuufuh, gulluh
4 kaan laazim tiHki ma3uh 3ashaan
5 bass tfuuz ilbaraziil

Arabic glossary

Unit 1

Word	Meaning	Arabic
ya	hey; a particle used to get someone's attention	يا
aaniseh (a+n+s)	Ms. (honorific term used for single women)	آنسة
biiki	with you	بيكي
shabaab (pl.) (sh+b+b)	guys (sing. = shab: young man; guy)	شباب
weyn	where	وين
3ind+i	have + I (this is a preposition, not a verb)	عندي
ma3+ak	have/with + you (masc. sing.)	معك
muHaaDHarah (H+aa+DH+r)	lecture	محاضرة
laazim (l+z+m)	must (this is a verbal noun: does not imply a doer)	لازم
ʔaruuH (r+w+H)	I go (the root is /r u H/)	اروح
bakkiir (b+k+r)	early (it is early)	بكير
yallah	(lit.) let's/let me (in this context, it means "OK")	يالله

Unit 2

Word	Meaning	Arabic
min	from	من
kamaan	again; too; another; more; besides	كمان
shukran	thanks	شكراً
itfaDDal	there you go (offering someone something)	تفضّل
ism+ii	name + my (my name)	اسمي
madiinah/madiinat (m+d+n)	city/town	مدينة
fi	in	في
bi+k+um	with + you + pl. (with you all)	بيكم

Unit 3

Word	Meaning	Arabic
shuuf (sh+w+f)	look! (masc. sing.)	شوف
miin	who?	مين
haay	this is (when referring to fem. sing.)	هاي
haadha	this is (when referring to masc. sing.)	هذا
maa shaa allaah	This is great!	ما شاء الله
Saghiir (S+gh+r)	small; young	صغير
kabiir (k+b+r)	big; old	كبير
Hilu (masc.); Hilwah (fem.)	good-looking; pretty	حلو
kthiir (k+th+r)	a lot	كثير
raaʔi3 (r+w+3)	wonderful (**raaʔi3ah** [fem.])	رائع
mumkin	possible (is it possible?)	ممكن
a3arrfak 3ala (3+r+r+f)	to introduce someone to	اعرفك على
3eilti (3eilih+i)	family + my (my family)	عيلتي
shuu	what	شو
dars (d+r+s)	lesson	درس
ʔadab (a+d+b)	literature	ادب

Word	Meaning	Arabic
bukrah (b+k+r)	tomorrow	بكره
yoom (y+w+m)	day	يوم
riyaaDah (r+y+D)	sports	رياضة
ʔakiid (a+k+d)	certainly	اكيد
Saff (S+f+f)	class	صف
SaHiiH (S+H+H)	right	صحيح
mumtaaz	excellent	ممتاز
3uTlah (3+T+T+l)	vacation; day off; break	عطلة
ʔayaam	days	ايام
kull	every	كل
ʔawwal (a+w+l)	first	اول
ʔaaxir (a+x+r)	last	اخير
shaari3	street	شارع
maktab (k+t+b)	office	مكتب
maktabah	library	مكتبة
miin	who?	مين
ma; maa	what?	ما
fiih	there (*exists*)	فيه

Unit 4

Word	Meaning	Arabic
laa; la	no	لا
maa; ma	no; not	ما
mish	not	مش
-iish	-not	يش
mabsuuT (b+s+T)	happy	مبسوط
ʔafTarit (f+T+r)	to have breakfast	افطار
bidd+/badd+ak	like to; want to	بد ك
tamaam (t+m+m)	fine; great; OK; wonderful	تمام
saa3ah (pl. saa3aat)	hour; watch	ساعة
maT3am (T+3+m)	restaurant	مطعم
aah	OK; I see	اه
maashi (m+sh+y)	sure; OK (will do); agree	ماشي
hnaak/hunaak/hinaak	there	هناك

Word	Meaning	Arabic
ma3 issalaamih (s+l+m)	goodbye (lit. with safety)	مع السلامة
hala	welcome; more endearment than "ahleyn"	هلا
3milti (3+m+l)	to do; to make	عملتي
ghada	lunch	غداء
btiSalu (w+S+l)	to arrive	بتصلو
halla?	now; soon	هلأ
ysallmik (s+l+m)	to protect: to save	يسلمك

Unit 5

Word	Meaning	Arabic
garSoon	waiter	قرصون
abu ishshabaab	buddy	ابو الشباب
SaHin	plate; dish	صحن
HummuS	hummus	حمص
fuul	fava beans	فول
Habbah; Habbih (pl. Habbaat)	piece, pieces	حبه
falaafil	falafel	فلافل
tikram (k+r+m)	with all generosity	تكرم
shay	tea	شاي
gahwah (?ahwih)	coffee	قهوه
bibsi	Pepsi (could be used for any cola drink product)	بيبسي
mayyih; may	water	ميه
law samaHt (s+m+H)	please, if you wish	لو سمحت
sukkar	sugar	سكر
zyaadih (z+y+d)	extra	زياده
HaaDir (H+D+r)	sure; will do	حاضر
tfaDDal? (f+D+l)	how can I help you?	تفضل
ay	any	اي
shi	thing	شي
thaani	second; else; other; another	ثاني
Hsaab (H+s+b)	check	حساب
dinaar (pl. dananiir)	dinar; dinars	دينار
SiHteyn	with health	صحتين

Word	Meaning	Arabic
3ala galbak	same to you (lit. to your heart)	على قلبك
bi+tu?muru (a+m+r)	to order; what do you order	بتأمرو
il+minyu	the menu	المنيو
bi+3yuun+i (3eyn; pl. 3yuun)	sure (lit. with my eyes)	بيعيوني
mashaawi (sh+w+a)	grilled meat	مشاوي
mshakkal (sh+k+k+l)	mixed	مشكل
salaTah (pl. salaTaat)	salad	سلطة
muqabilaat (no sing. form)	appetizers	مقبلات
mtabbal	mashed zucchini; mashed eggplant	متبل
Haarrah	spicy; hot	حارة
mHammarah	mashed hot pepper	محمرة
kibbih	meat-stuffed bulgur balls	كبة
laban	yogurt; sour cream	لبن
mxlallal; mxallalaat	pickles	مخلل
taHit amrik	at your disposal (lit. under your order)	تحت امرك
sheysh jaaj	grilled chicken skewers	شيش جاج
dagiigah (pl. dagaayig)	minute; minutes	دقيقة
wasaT	medium	وسط
biitza	pizza	بيتزا
maragriita	Margherita, vegetarian pizza	مارجريتا
bass	only	بس
xuDaar (x+D+r)	vegetables	خضار
fiTir; fuTur; mashruum	mushroom	فطر
zeytuun	olives	زيتون
Hajim	size	حجم
nuSS	half	نص
mushkilih (pl. mashaakil)	problem	مشكلة
hadool	these	هدول
3inwaan+ak	your address	عنوانك
shagah (pl. shugag)	apartment	شقة
3amaarah; 3amaarit (pl. 3amaaraat)	building	عمارة
shaari3 (pl. shawaari3)	street	شارع
3ala Tuul	sure, certainly	على طول
b+akuun (k+aa+n)	to be	بكون

Unit 6

Word	Meaning	Arabic
yislamu	may (your hands) be well	يسلمو
mansaf	a plate of rice, lamb or chicken and yogurt soup	منسف
ybaarik fi (b+r+k)	to bless someone or something	يبارك
ghallabtu (gh+l+l+b)	to go to the trouble of; inconvenience someone	غلبتو
Haalkum	yourselves	حالكم
ʔabadan	not at all; never	ابداً
ghalabih (n.)	inconvenience	غلبة
bism illaah	in the name of God	بسم الله
il+ʔakil (a+k+l)	food	الأكل
bi+jannin (j+n+n)	to make crazy (crazy good)	بيجنن
al+Hamdu (H+m+d)	to praise	الحمد
ziid (z+y+d)	to add or do something more	زيد
kul (a+k+l)	eat (v. imperative)	كُل
wallah	I swear by God	والله
shbi3it (sh+b+3)	to feel full (of food)	شبعت
sufrah	dining; the act of dining	سُفره
daaymih (d+w+m)	continuous; always present	دايمة
mniiHah	good, well	منيحة
ʔasaʔlik (s+ʔ+l)	I ask you	أسألك
bitHibbi (H+b+b)	you (fem.) like	بتحبي
3ashaʔ	dinner	عشاء
Habiibti	my darling	حبيبتي
b+SaraaHah	frankly	بصراحة
nabaatiyyih (nabaati+fem.)	vegetarian	نباتية
baakul (ʔ+k+l)	to eat	باكل
laHmih	meat (red meat)	لحمة
jaaj	chicken (white meat)	جاج
maashi	OK, fine, sure	ماشي
raayiH (r+w+H)	to go	رايح
faaSuulyia	(Italian) white beans	فاصوليا

Word	Meaning	Arabic
xuDaar	vegetables	خضار
mshakkalih (mshakkal+fem.)	mixed	مشكلة
samak	fish	سمك
kamaan	again, besides, in addition to	كمان
3adas	lentils	عدس
bandoorah	tomatoes	بندوره
bass heyk	just that	بس هيك
ba3deyn	later	بعدين
niHki 3an (H+k+y 3an)	to talk about	نحكي عن
xuTat (pl. xuTatT)	plan	خطة
nashaaTaat (sing. nashaaT)	activities	نشاطات
barnaamij (pl. baraamij)	program	برنامج
bibda? (b+d+?)	to start	ببدأ
ziyaarat (sing. ziyaarah)	visits	زيارة
riHlih (pl. riHlaat)	trip	رحلة
3iid	festival	عيد
ilaDHa	sacrifice	الأضحى
3iid ilaDHa	Eid Al-Adha (The Festival of Sacrifice)	عيد الأضحى
Tayyib	OK, sure	طيب
ray (pl. aaraa?)	opinion	راي
fikrah (pl. afkaar)	idea	فكره
imtiHaanaat (sing. imtiHaan)	test, exam	امتحانات

Unit 7

Word	Meaning	Arabic
kaasih (pl. kaasaat)	glass	كاسه
funjaan (pl. fanajiin)	cup	فنجان
ʔargiilih (pl. ʔaraagiil)	hookah	ارجيله
yxaliik (x+l+l+y)	to keep, to leave, to let go	يخليك
na3na3	mint	نعنع
saada	sugar-free	سادة
nakha (pl. nakhaat)	flavor	نكهة
tuffaaHah (pl. tuffaaH)	apple	تفاح
faraawlih	strawberry	فراولة
leymuun	lemon	ليمون
shummaam	melons	شمام
zabbiTT-ha (z+b+T)	to fix; to do something well	زبطها
badaxxin (d+x+x+n)	to smoke	بدخن
aHsan+li	better for	احسنلي
twaSilni (w+S+S+l)	to give a ride to; to deliver	توصلني
iTla3i (T+l+3)	to ride up; to become	اطلعي
3inwaan (pl. 3anawiin)	address	عنوان
jariidih (pl. jaraayid)	newspaper	جريدة
shaari3 (pl. shawaari3)	street	شارع
raʔiisi	main	رئيسي
sawwaag (pl. sawwaagiin)	driver	سواق
jdiid or jadiid	new	جديد
binaayih (pl. binaayaat)	building	بناية
Hawaali	almost	حوالي
mitir (pl. mtaar)	meter	متر
(duuz) dughri	straight	دغري
3rift (3+r+f)	to know	عرفت
daxlih (pl. daxlaat)	side street	دخله
ʔujrah	(taxi) fare	اجره
nishrab (sh+r+b)	to drink	نشرب
ʔamiiS or gamiiS	shirt	قميص
shiik	elegant; good-looking	شيك
mitl or mitil	like, similar to	متل
nafs	same as	نفس

Word	Meaning	Arabic
ishtareytiih (?+sh+t+r+y)	to buy	اشتريتيه
jaabatuh (j+y+b)	to bring	جابته
hadiyyih (pl. hadaaya)	gift	هدية
taman or thaman	price	تمن
ya3ni (3+n+y)	to mean; it means	يعني
mashghuul	busy	مشغول
Sayydalliiyih (pl. Sayydalliiyaat)	pharmacy	صيدلية
Haraarah	fever	حرارة
mawjuud	available	موجود
miin	who (lamin: for whom?)	مين
dawa (pl. ?adwiyih)	medication	دواء
?ibn (pl. ?abnaa)	son	ابن
3umr (pl. a3maar)	age	عمر
sanih (pl. sniin)	year	سنه
salaamih	wellness; peace	سلامه
rubu3 (pl. rbaa3)	quarter	ربع
?ajnabi (pl. ajaanib)	foreign; foreigner	اجنبي
si3r (pl. as3aar)	price	سعر
jaahiz	ready	جاهز

Unit 8

Word	Meaning	Arabic
Sa3b	difficult	صعب
y3iinik (3+w+n)	to help, to support	يعينك
taxaSSuS (pl. taxaSSuSaat)	specialization	تخصص
Tawiil	tall, long, takes a long time	طويل
shughul	work	شغل
mawjuud	available	موجود
taxarruj (t+x+x+r+j)	graduation	تخرج
SaHiiH	correct, right	صحيح
ywafgik (w+f+g)	to help achieve one's goals	يوفقك
wara	behind	وراء
ba3DH	some	بعض

Word	Meaning	Arabic
heyk	this/for this reason	هيك
bi3iin (3+w+n)	to help	بيعين
yiTla3	to become; to turn out to be	يطلع
naawi (n+w+y)	to intend to, to plan to	ناوي
titghadda (gh+d+d)	to have lunch	تتغدى
faraagh (pl. faraaghaat)	free time	فراغ
ghada	lunch	غداء
Hsaab (pl. Hsaabaat)	account	حسب
waajib (pl. waajibaat)	duty	واجب
ysallmak (s+l+l+m)	to keep (one) at peace	يسلمك
mTawwil (T+w+l)	taking it/him a long time to (arrive)	مطول
baaS (pl. baaSaat)	bus	باص
raH	will	رح
nit?axxar (?+x+x+r)	to be late; to come late	نتأخر
yuuSal (w+S+l)	to arrive	يوصل
sur3ah	fast	سرعة
?azmih (pl. ?azmaat)	traffic jam; crowded	أزمة
nilHag (l+H+g)	to catch (a bus, someone, an appointment)	نلحق
makaan (pl. amaakin)	place	مكان
idha	if	اذا
isma3 (s+m+3)	to hear	اسمع
yiiji (j+?+y)	to come; to arrive	ييجي
shubbaak (pl. shababiik)	window	شباك
leysh	why	ليش
3alashaan	because	علشان
tiHjiz (H+j+z)	to reserve	تحجز
ti3Ti (3+T+y)	to give	تعطي
kursi (pl. karaasi)	chair	كرسي
ba3malha (3+m+l)	to do; to make	بعملها
txaaf (x+w+f)	to fear	تخاف
niswanji	womanizer; loves women	نسونجي
ysaamiH (s+m+H)	to forgive	يسامح

Unit 9

Word	Meaning	Arabic
?ashtari (sh+t+r)	to buy	أشتري
shaal (pl. shaalaat)	scarf	شال
xaatim (pl. xawaatim)	ring	خاتم
fiDDah (n.)	silver	فضة
loon (pl. alwaan)	color	لون
saada (adj.)	one color	سادة
mzarkash (adj.)	embroidered	مزركش
?aSli (adj.)	original	أصلي
ghaali (adj.)	expensive	غالي
aHsan (adj.)	better	أحسن
3alashaan	because	علشان
ray+ak	your opinion	رايك
raas maal	prime cost	راس مال
lissa	yet	لسا
mabrook/mubaarak	congratulations	مبروك
badawwir 3ala (d+w+w+r)	to look for; search for	بدور على
mudeyl (pl. mudeylaat)	fashion; style	موديل
banTaloon (pl. banaTiil)	trousers, pants	بنطلون
jiinz	jeans	جينز
mgallam	striped	مقلم
balbis (l+b+s)	to wear	بلبس
laarj	large	لارج
gyaas (pl. gyaasaat)	size	قياس
maSaari	money	مصاري
raa3ii (r+3+y)	to take care of someone	راعي
guTin	cotton	قطن
Siini	Chinese	صيني
suuri	Syrian	سوري
si3ir or thaman	price	سعر

Unit 10

Word	Meaning	Arabic
su?aal (pl. ?as?ilih)	question	سؤال
markiz (pl. maraakiz)	center	مركز
SiHi	healthy (markiz SiHi: health clinic)	صحي
bizzabT	exactly	بالزبط
galluulak (g+w+l)	to say; to tell	قالولك
bilaagiik (l+g+y)	to find	بيلاقيك
maHal (pl. maHallaat)	store	محل
bley steyshin	PlayStation	بلاي ستيشن
zaawyih (pl. zawaaya)	corner	زاوية
Taabig (pl. Tawaabig)	floor	طابق
baarak (b+r+k)	to bless	بارك
waja3 (pl. awjaa3)	pain	وجع
sinn (pl. asnaan)	teeth	سن
?ay	which	أي
jabal ittaaj	Jabal Altaaj (place name)	جبل التاج
ijtimaa3 (pl. ijtimaa3aat)	meeting	اجتماع
3aSr	evening time	عصر
nzuur (z+aa+r)	to visit	نزور
maw3id (pl. mawaa3iid)	appointment	موعد
ajaddid (j+d+d)	to renew	أجدد
iqaamah (pl. iqaamaat)	residency	إقامة
xallSi (x+l+l+S)	to finish	خلصي
fawaakih	fruit	فواكة
xuDaar	vegetables	خضار
Taaza	fresh (food, drink)	طازة
raxiiS	cheap	رخيص
sha3r	hair	شعر
aHDar (H+D+r)	to watch (a movie)	أحضر
SaaHib (pl. SHaab)	friend (male)	صاحب
SaaHbih (pl. SaaHbaat)	friend (female)	صاحبه

Unit 11

Word	Meaning	Arabic
ta3baan	tired	تعبان
Haass	feeling (I'm feeling)	حاسّ
wajji3ni (w+j+3)	to hurt	يجرح
jisim (pl. ajsaam)	body	جسم
xafiif	light; moderate; not severe	خفيف
maghiS	stomach ache	مغص
naDiif	clean	نظيف
halla?	now	هلا
daayix	dizzy	دايخ
dooxah	dizziness	دوخة
Ha? (Hag)	right	حق
shadiid	strong, severe	شديد
ghalaT	wrong	غلط
ruzz	rice	رز
Hammaam (pl. Hammamaat)	bathroom	حمّام
ya3ni	almost	يعني
xalli (x+l+l+y)	to let	خلّي
meyrameyyih	sage	ميرمية
bitSiiri (S+y+r)	to become	بتصيري

Unit 12

Word	Meaning	Arabic
nihaayih (pl. nihaayaat)	end	نهاية (ج. نهايات)
?usboo3 (pl. asaabii3)	week	اسبوع
ya3ni	so	يعني
darajih (pl. darajaat)	step; degree	درجة
fi3lan	truly, for sure	فعلاً
?afakkir (f+k+k+r)	to think	أفكر
mawDuu3 (pl. mawaaDii3)	topic, subject, issue	موضوع
nashaaT (pl. nashaaTaat)	activity	نشاط
Tab3an	of course	طبعاً
mahrajaan	festival	مهرجان
leyl	night time	ليل
zaHmih	crowded	زحمة
bariTaanya	Britain	بريطانيا
shab3aan	full of; has plenty of	شبعان

Unit 13

Word	Meaning	Arabic
titfarraj (f+r+r+j)	to watch	تتفرّج
riyal madriid	Real Madrid (football team)	ريال مدريد
barshaloonah	Barcelona (football team)	برشلونة
majnuun	crazy; out of your mind	مجنون
DHidd	against	ضد
mihtamm	interested	مهتم
?uroobiyyih	European	أوروبية
Haarah (pl. Haaraat)	neighborhood; quarter	حارة (ج. حارات)
za3laan	mad; angry	زعلان
aax!	ouch!; alas	آخ
mawsim (pl. mawaasim)	season	موسم (ج. مواسم)
ilfeySali	Al-Faisali, Jordanian soccer team	الفيصلي
thaalaath waaHad	three to one	ثلاثة – واحد

Word	Meaning	Arabic
SaaliH	in favor of; for	صالح
ilwiHdaat	Al-Wihdat, Jordanian soccer team	الوحدات
basiiTah	easy; not a problem	بسيطة
marrah (pl. marraat)	one time; once	مرة (ج. مرات)
nihaaʔi	final	نهائي
agullik (g+w+l)	to say	أقلك
daxal (d+x+l)	to enter	دخل
ʔasaas	basis	أساس
balaash (+verb)	there is no need to	بلاش
Saar li	it has been (time)	صار لي
shughul	job	شغل
3ilm (pl. 3uluum)	science	علم (ج. علوم)
siyaasih (pl. syaasaat)	politics; policy	سياسة (ج. سياسات)
ʔistanna (ʔ+s+t+n+y)	to wait	استنّى
faaydih (pl. fawaaʔid)	profit, benefit	فايدة (ج. فوائد)
ishtaghalu (sh+gh+l)	to work	اشتغلوا
waasTah (pl. waasTaat)	mediation; middleman	واسطة (ج. واسطات)
door (pl. ʔadwaar)	line; turn	دور (ج. أدوار)
naaxudh (ʔ+x+dh)	to take	ناخذ
ittiSaal (pl. ittiSaalaat)	call; phone call	اتصال (ج. اتصالات)

English glossary

A

account	حساب	Hsaab (pl. Hsaabaat)
activities	نشاطات	nashaaTaat (sing. nashaaT)
to add or do something more	زيد	ziid (z+y+d)
address	عنوان	3inwaan (pl. 3anawiin)
again, besides, in addition to	كمان	kamaan
against	ضد	DHidd
age	عُمُر	3umr (pl. a3maar)
Al-Faisali, Jordanian soccer team	الفيصلي	ilfeySali
almost	يعني ;حوالي	Hawaali; ya3ni
Al-Wihdat, Jordanian soccer team	الوحدات	ilwiHdaat
any	أي	?ay
apartment	شقة	shagah (pl. shugag)
appetizers	مقبلات	muqabilaat (no sing. form)
apple	تفاح	tuffaaHah (pl. tuffaaH)
appointment	موعد	maw3id (pl. mawaa3iid)
to arrive	يوصَل ;بتِصلو	btiSalu (w+S+l); yuuSal (w+S+l)
at your disposal (lit. under your order)	تحت امرك	taHit amrik
available	موجود	mawjuud

B

Barcelona (football team)	برشلونة	barshaloonah
basis	أساس	?asaas (pl. ?asaasaat)
bathroom	حمّام	Hammaam: (pl. Hammamaat)
to be	بكون	b+akuun (k+aa+n)
to be late; to come late	نتأخر	nit?axxar (?+x+x+r)

because	علشان	3alashaan
to become; to turn out to be	يطلع ;بتصيري	bitSiiri: (S+y+r); yiTla3
behind	وراء	wara
better	أحسن	?aHsan (adj.)
better for	أحسنلي	?aHsan+li
big; old	كبير	kabiir (k+b+r)
to bless; to bless someone or something	يبارك ;بارك	baarak (b+r+k); ybaarik fi (b+r+k)
body	جسم	jisim (pl. ajsaam)
to bring	جابته	jaabatuh (j+y+b)
Britain	بريطانيا	bariTaanya
buddy	ابو الشباب	abu ishshabaab
building	عمارة ;بناية	binaayih (pl. binaayaat); 3amaarah; 3amaarit (pl. 3amaaraat)
bus	باص	baaS (pl. baaSaat)
busy	مشغول	mashghuul
to buy	أشتري ;اشتريتيه	ishtareytiih (?+sh+t+r+y); ?ashtari (sh+t+r)

c

call; phone call	اتصال	ittiSaal (pl. ittiSaalaat)
to catch (a bus, someone, an appointment)	نلحق	nilHag (l+H+g)
center	مركز	markiz (pl. maraakiz)
certainly	اكيد	?akiid (a+k+d)
chair	كرسي	kursi (pl. karaasi)
cheap	رخيص	raxiiS
check	حساب	Hsaab (H+s+b)
chicken (white meat)	جاج	jaaj
Chinese	صيني	Siini
city/town	مدينه	madiinah/madiinat (m+d+n) (pl. mudun)
class	صف	Saff (S+f+f) (pl. Sufuuf)
clean	نظيف	naDiif
coffee	قهوه	gahwah (?ahwih)
color	لون	loon (pl. alwaan)
to come; to arrive	بيجي	yiiji (j+?+y)
congratulations	مبروك	mabrook/mubaarak
continuous; always present	دايمة	daayimih (d+w+m)
corner	زاوية	zaawyih (pl. zawaaya)
correct, right	صحيح	SaHiiH (S+H+H)

cotton	قطن	**guTin**
crazy; out of your mind	مجنون	**majnuun (pl. majaaniin)**
crowded	زحمة	**zaHmih**
cup	فنجان	**funjaan (pl. fanajiin)**

D

day	يوم	**yoom (y+w+m)**
		(pl. ?ayaam)
difficult	صعب	**Sa3b**
dinar; dinars	دينار	**dinaar (pl. dananiir)**
dining; the act of dining	سُفره	**sufrah**
dinner	عشاء	**3asha?**
dizziness	دوخة	**dooxah**
dizzy	دايخ	**daayix**
to do; to make	عملتي ;بعملها	**ba3malha (3+m+l);**
		3milti (3+m+l)
to drink	نشرب	**nishrab (sh+r+b)**
driver	سواق	**sawwaag (pl. sawwaagiin)**
duty	واجب	**waajib (pl. waajibaat)**

E

early (it is early)	بكير	**bakkiir (b+k+r)**
easy; not a problem	بسيطه	**basiiTah**
eat (v. imperative)	كُل	**kul (?a+k+l)**
to eat	باكل	**baakul (?+k+l)**
Eid Al-Adha (The Festival of	عيد الأضحى	**3iid il?aDHa**
Sacrifice)		
elegant; good-looking	شيك	**shiik**
embroidered	مزركش	**mzarkash (adj.)**
end	نهاية	**nihaayih (pl. nihaayaat)**
to enter	دخله	**daxal (d+x+l)**
European	أوروبية	**?uroobiyyih**
evening time	عصر	**3aSr**
every	كل	**kull**
exactly	بالزبط	**bizzabT**
excellent	مقبلات	**mumtaaz**
expensive	غالي	**ghaali (adj.)**
extra	زياده	**zyaadih (z+y+d)**

F

falafel	فلافل	**falaafil**
family + my (my family)	عيلتي	**3eilti (3eilih+i)**

fare (taxi)	أجره	?ujrah
fashion; style	موديل	mudeyl (pl. mudeylaat)
fast	سرعة	sur3ah
fava beans	فول	fuul
to fear	تخاف	txaaf (x+w+f)
to feel full (of food)	شبعت	shbi3it (sh+b+3)
feeling (I'm feeling)	حاس	Haass
festival	مهرجان; عيد	mahrajaan (pl. mahrajaanaat); 3iid
fever	حرارة	Haraarah
final	نهائي	nihaa?i
to find	بيلاقيك	bilaagiik (l+g+y)
fine; great; OK; wonderful	تمام	tamaam (t+m+m)
to finish	خلصي	xallSi (x+l+l+S)
first	أول	?awwal (a+w+l)
fish	سمك	samak
to fix; to do something well	زبطها	zabbiTT-ha (z+b+T)
flavor	نكهة	nakhaha (pl. nakhaat)
floor	طابق	Taabig (pl. Tawaabig)
food	الأكل	il+?akil (?a+k+l)
foreign; foreigner	أجنبي	?ajnabi (pl. ajaanib)
to forgive	يسامح	ysaamiH (s+m+H)
frankly	بصراحة	b+SaraaHah
free time	فراغ	faraagh (pl. faraaghaat)
fresh (food, drink)	طازة	Taaza
friend (female)	صاحبه	SaaHbih (pl. SaaHbaat)
friend (male)	صاحب	SaaHib (pl. SHaab)
from	من	min
fruit	فواكة	fawaakih
full of; has plenty of	شبعان	shab3aan

G

gift	هدية	hadiyyih (pl. hadaaya)
to give	تعطي	ti3Ti (3+T+y)
to give a ride to; to deliver	توصلني	twaSilni (w+S+S+l)
glass	كاسه	kaasih (pl. kaasaat)
to go	رايح	raayiH (r+w+H)
to go to the trouble of; inconvenience someone	غلبتو	ghallabtu (gh+l+l+b)
good, well	منيحة	mniiHah
good-bye (lit. with safety)	مع السلامة	ma3 issalaamih (s+l+m)
good-looking; pretty	حلو	Hilu (masc.); Hilwah (fem.)

graduation	تخرج	taxarruj (t+x+x+r+j)
grilled chicken skewers	شيش جاج	sheysh jaaj
grilled meat	مشغول	mashaawi (sh+w+a)
guys (sing. = **shab**: young man; guy)	شب	shab (pl. shabaab) (sh+b+b)

H

hair	شعر	sha3r
half	نص	nuSS
happy	مبسوط	mabsuuT (b+s+T)
have + I (this is a preposition, not a verb)	عندي	3ind+i
to have breakfast	أفطرت	?afTarit (f+T+r)
to have lunch	تتغدى	titghadda (gh+d+d)
have/with + you (masc. sing.)	معك	ma3+ak
healthy (**markiz SiHi**: health clinic)	صحي	SiHi
to hear	اسمع	isma3 (s+m+3)
to help, to support	يعينك ;بيعين	bi3iin (3+w+n); y3iinik (3+w+n)
to help achieve one's goals	يوفقك	ywafgik (w+f+g)
hey; a particle used to get someone's attention	يا	ya
hookah	ارجيله	?argiilih (pl. ?araagiil)
hour; watch	ساعة	saa3ah (pl. saa3aat)
how can I help you	تفضل	tfaDDal
hummus	حمص	HummuS
to hurt	وَجّعني	wajji3ni (w+j+3)

I

I ask you	أسألك	?asa?lik (s+?+l)
I go (the root is /r u H/)	اروح	?aruuH (r+w+H)
I swear by God	والله	wallah
idea	فكرة	fikrah (pl. afkaar)
if	اذا	idha
in	في	fi
in favor of; for	صالح	SaaliH
in the name of God	بسم الله	bism illaah
inconvenience	غلبة	ghalabih (n.)
to intend to, to plan to	ناوي	naawi (n+w+y)
interested	مهتم	mihtamm

| to introduce to | اعرفك على | a3arrfak 3ala (3+r+f) |
| it has been (time) | صارلي | Saar li |

J

Jabal Altaaj (place name)	جبل التاج	jabal ittaaj
jeans	جينز	jiinz
just that	بس هيك	bass heyk

K

to keep (one) at peace	يسلمك	ysallmak (s+l+l+m)
to keep, to leave, to let go	يخليك	yxaliik (x+l+l+y)
to know	عرفت	3rift (3+r+f)

L

large	لارج	laarj
later	بعدين	ba3deyn
lecture	محاضرة	muHaaDHarah (H+aa+DH+r) (pl. muHaDHarrat)
lemon	ليمون	leymuun
lentils	عدس	3adas
lesson	درس	dars (d+r+s) (pl. duruus)
to let	خلّي	xalli: (x+l+l+y)
(lit.) let's/let me; (in this context, it means, OK)	يالله	yallah
library	مكتبه	maktabah (pl. maktabaat)
light; moderate; not severe	خفيف	xafiif
like, similar to	متل	mitil or mitl
like to; want to	بدك	bidd+/badd+ak
line; turn	دور	door (pl. ʔadwaar)
literature	أدب	ʔadab (a+d+b) (pl. aadaab)
look! (masc. sing.)	شوف	shuuf (sh+w+f)
to look for; search for	بدور على	badawwir 3ala (d+w+w+r)
a lot	كثير	kthiir (k+th+r)
lunch	غداء	ghada

M

mad; angry	زعلان	za3laan
main	رئيسي	raʔiisi
to make crazy (crazy good)	بيجنن	bi+jannin (j+n+n)
margherita, vegetarian pizza	مارجريتا	margariita
mashed hot pepper	محمره	mHammarah

mashed zucchini; mashed eggplant	متبّل	mtabbal
may (your hands) be well	يسلمو	yislamu
to mean; it means	يعني	ya3ni (3+n+y)
meat (red meat)	لحمة	laHmih
meat-stuffed bulgur balls	كبّة	kibbih
mediation; middleman	واسطة	waasTah (pl. waasTaat)
medication	دواء	dawa (pl. ?adwiyih)
medium	وسط	wasaT
meeting	اجتماع امتحانات	ijtimaa3 (pl. ijtimaa3aat)
melons	شمّام	shummaam
the menu	المنيو	il+minyu
meter	متر	mitir (pl. mtaar)
mint	نعنع	na3na3
minute; minutes	دقيقة	dagiigah (pl. dagaayig)
mixed	مشكل	mshakkal (sh+k+k+l)
money	مصاري	maSaari
Ms. (honorific term used for single women)	آنسة	aaniseh (a+n+s) (pl. aanisaat)
mushroom	فطر	fiTir; fuTur; mashruum
must (this is a verbal noun: does not imply a doer)	لازم	laazim (l+z+m)
my darling	حبيبتي	Habiibti

N

name + my (my name)	اسمي	ism+ii
neighborhood; quarter	حارة	Haarah (pl. Haaraat)
new	جديد	jdiid or jadiid
newspaper	جريدة	jariidih (pl. jaraayid)
night time	ليل	leyl
no	لا	laa; la
no; not	ما	maa; ma
not	مش	mish
-not	بش	-iish
not at all; never	أبداً	?abadan
now; soon	هلأ	halla?

O

of course	طبعاً	Tab3an
office	مكتب	maktab (k+t+b) (pl. makaatib)

OK, fine, sure; I see	اه ؛طيب ؛ماشي	maashi (m+sh+y); Tayyib; aah
olives	زيتون	zeytuun
one color	سادة	saada (adj.)
one time; once	مرّه	marrah (pl. marraat)
only	بس	bass
opinion	راي	ray (pl. aaraaʔ)
to order; what do you order	بتأمرو	bi+tuʔmuru (ʔa+m+r)
original	أصلي	ʔaSli (adj.)
ouch!; alas!	اخ	aax!

P

pain	وجع	waja3 (pl. ʔawjaa3)
Pepsi (could be used for any cola drink product)	بيبسي	bibsi
pharmacy	صيدلية	Sayydalliiyih (pl. Sayydalliiyaat)
pickles	مخلل	mxlallal; mxallalaat
piece, pieces	حبه	Habbah; Habbih (pl. Habbaat)
pizza	بيتزا	biitza
place	مكان	makaan (pl. amaakin)
plan	خطة	xuTat (pl. xuTatT)
plate; dish	صحن	SaHin
a plate of rice, lamb or chicken and yogurt soup	منسف	mansaf (pl. manaasif)
PlayStation	بلاي ستيشن	bley steyshin
please, if you wish	لو سمحت	law samaHt (s+m+H)
politics; policy	سياسة	siyaasih (pl. syaasaat)
possible (is it possible?)	ممكن	mumkin
to praise	الحمد	il+Hamdu (H+m+d)
price	تمن ؛سعر	si3r (pl. as3aar); taman or thaman
prime cost	راس مال	raas maal
problem	مشكله	mushkilih (pl. mashaakil)
profit, benefit	فايدة	faaydih (pl. fawaaʔid)
program	برنامج	barnaamij (pl. baraamij)
to protect: to save	يسلمك	ysallmik (s+l+m)

Q

quarter	رُبع	rubu3 (pl. rbaa3)
question	سؤال	suʔaal (pl. ʔasʔilih)

R

ready	جاهز	jaahiz
Real Madrid (football team)	ريال مدريد	riyal madriid
to renew	أجدد	ajaddid (j+d+d)
to reserve	تحجز	tiHjiz (H+j+z)
residency	اقامه	iqaamah (pl. iqaamaat)
restaurant	مطعم	maT3am (T+3+m) (pl. maTaa3im)
rice	رَز	ruzz
to ride up; to become	اطلعي	iTla3i (T+l+3)
right	حق	Hag (Ha?)
ring	خاتم	xaatim (pl. xawaatim)

S

sacrifice	الأضحى	il?aDHa
sage	ميرميه	meyrameyyih
salad	سلطة	salaTah (pl. salaTaat)
same as	نفس	nafs
same to you (lit. to your heart)	على قلبك	3ala galbak
to say; to tell	قالولك; أقُلَّك	agullik (g+w+l); galluulak (g+w+l)
scarf	شال	shaal (pl. shaalaat)
science	عِلم	3ilm (pl. 3uluum)
season	موعد	mawsim (pl. mawaasim)
second; else; other; another	ثاني	thaani
shirt	قميص	?amiiS or gamiiS
side street	دخله	daxlih (pl. daxlaat)
silver	فضة	fiDDah (n.)
size	قياس; حجم	Hajim; gyaas (pl. gyaasaat)
small; young	صغير	Saghiir (S+gh+r)
to smoke	بدخن	badaxxin (d+x+x+n)
so	يعني	ya3ni
some	بعض	ba3DH
son	ابن	?ibn (pl. ?abnaa)
specialization	تخصص	taxaSSuS (pl. taxaSSuSaat)
spicy; hot	حارّة	Haarrah
sport	رياضة	riyaaDah (r+y+D) (pl. riyaaDaat)
to start	ببدأ	bibda? (b+d+?)
step; degree	درجة	darajih (pl. darajaat)
stomach ache	مغص	maghiS

store	محلّ	maHal (pl. maHallaat)
straight	دغري	dughri (duuz)
strawberry	فراولة	faraawlih
street	شارع	shaari3 (pl. shawaari3)
striped	مقلّم	mgallam
strong, severe	شديد	shadiid
sugar	سكر	sukkar
sugar-free	سادة	saada
sure, certainly; sure (lit. with my eyes); will do	على طول؛ بعيوني؛ حاضر	3ala Tuul; bi+3yuun+i (3eyn; pl. 3yuun); HaaDir (H+D+r)
Syrian	سوري	suuri

T

to take	ناخذ	naaxudh (?+x+dh)
to take care of someone	رائع	raa3ii (r+3+y)
taking it/him a long time to (arrive)	مطوّل	mTawwil (T+w+l)
to talk about	نحكي عن	niHki 3an (H+k+y 3an)
tall, long, takes a long time	طويل	Tawiil
tea	شاي	shay
teeth	سن	sinn (pl. ?asnaan)
test, exam	إمتحانات	imtiHaanaat (sing. imtiHaan)
thanks	شكراً	shukran
there	هناك	hnaak/hunaak/hinaak
there (exists)	فيه	fiih
there is no need to	بلاش	balaash (+verb)
there you go (offering someone something)	تفضّل	tfaDDal
these	هدول	hadool
thing	شي	shi
to think	أفكّر	?afakkir (f+k+k+r)
this/for this reason	هيك	heyk
this is (when referring to fem. sing.)	هاي	haay
this is (when referring to masc. sing.)	هذا	haadha
This is great!	ما شاء الله	maa shaa allaah
three to one	ثلاث ـ واحد	thaalaath waaHad
tired	تعبان	ta3baan
tomatoes	بندوره	bandoorah

tomorrow	بكره	bukrah (b+k+r)
topic, subject, issue	موضوع	mawDuu3 (pl. mawaaDii3)
traffic jam; crowded	أزمة	?azmih (pl. ?azmaat)
trip	رحله	riHlih (pl. riHlaat)
trousers, pants	بنطلون	banTaloon (pl. banaTiil)
truly, for sure	فعلاً	fi3lan

V

vacation; day off; break	عطلة	3uTlah (3+T+l)(pl. 3uTal)
vegetables	خضار	xuDaar (x+D+r)
vegetarian	نباتية	nabaatiyyih (nabaati+fem.)
visit	زيارة	ziyaarat (sing. ziyaarah)
to visit	نزور	nzuur (z+aa+r)

W

to wait	إستنى	?istanna (?+s+t+n+y)
waiter	قرصون	garSoon
to watch; to watch (a movie)	أحضر؛تتفرج	titfarraj (f+r+r+j); aHDar (H+D+r)
water	ميه	mayyih; may (pl. miyaah)
to wear	بلبس	balbis (l+b+s)
week	أسبوع	?usboo3 (pl. asaabii3)
welcome; more endearment than "ahleyn"	هلا	hala
wellness; peace	سلامة	salaamih
what	شو	shuu
what?	ما	ma; maa
where	وين	weyn
which	أي	?ay
(Italian) white beans	فاصوليا	faaSuulyia
who	مش	miin
why	ليش	leysh
will	رَح	raH
window	شباك	shubbaak (pl. shababiik)
with all generosity	تكرم	tikram (k+r+m)
with health	صحتين	SiHteyn
with you	بيكي	biiki
with + you + pl. (with you all)	بيكم	bi+k+um
womanizer; loves women	نسونجي	niswanji
wonderful (**raa?i3ah** [fem.])	رائع	raa?i3 (r+w+3)
work; job	شغل	shughul
to work	اشتغلو	ishtaghalu (sh+gh+l)
wrong	غلط	ghalaT

Y

year	سنة	**sanih (pl. sniin)**
yet	لسا	**lissa**
yogurt; sour cream	لبن	**laban**
you (fem.) like	بتحبي	**bitHibbi (H+b+b)**
your address	عنوانك	**3inwaan+ak**
your opinion	رايك	**ray+ak**
yourselves	حالكم	**Haalkum**

Answer key

Transliteration key

Exercise 2

1 Lebanon
2 Syria
3 Jordan
4 Palestine
5 Israel

6 Libya
7 Italy
8 France
9 Kuwait

Exercise 3

ا	ب	ت	ث	ج
129	25	31	6	7
ح	خ	د	ذ	ر
13	3	23	5	45
ز	س	ش	ص	ض
7	13	12	5	12
ط	ظ	ع	غ	ف
7	4	20	2	20
ق	ك	ل	م	ن
12	11	75	44	38
ه	و	ي		
10	35	50		

Unit 1

Exercise 1

1 wa a`laykum assa`laam
2 Sa`baaH in`noor; Sa`baaH il`ward
3 `ana min lubnaan
4 al`Hamdu lil`laah; ta`maam; `kwayyis
5 al`Hamdu lil`laah

Exercise 2

1 ma`saa in`noor; ma`saa il`ward
2 `kiif<u>ik</u>?; `kiifak?
3 `marHaba
4 `ahlan wa `sahlan; `tsharrafna; `winni3im
5 `ana + (name)
6 al`Hamdu lil`laah; ta`maam
7 Sa`baaH il`xeyr
8 `intah/`inti min weyn?
9 `kiif/`keyf il`Haal?
10 `ahlan wa `sahlan; ah`lein; ya `hala

Exercise 3

1 kaasha
2 kaasi
3 kaasna
4 kaasuh
5 kaashum
6 kaashin
7 kaasak
8 kaasik
9 kaaskum
10 kaaskum

Exercise 4

1	`galam<u>na</u>	our pen
2	`galam<u>ak</u>	your (sing. masc.) pen
3	`galam<u>ik</u>	your (sing. fem.) pen
4	`galam<u>ku</u>; `galam<u>kum</u> (pl. masc.)	your pen
5	`galam<u>ku</u>; `galam<u>kum</u> (pl. fem.)	your pen
6	`galam<u>uh</u>	his pen
7	`galam<u>ha</u>	her pen
8	`galam<u>hum</u>	their (pl. masc.) pen
9	`galam<u>hin</u>	their (pl. fem.) pen

Exercise 5

1 ilwalad; alwalad	5 izzeit; alzayt
2 ilbinit; albint	6 liHmaar; alHimaar
3 ilxubiz; ilxubz	7 lislaaH; assilaaH
4 iddaar; addaar	8 ishshabaab; ashshabaab

Exercise 6

1 `baab kbiir	6 mu`handisih ga`Siir
2 kaasih kbiirih	7 `baab Sghiir
3 `m3allim Ta`wiil	8 binit Ta`wiileh
4 `m3allimih Ta`wiileh	9 bait kbiir
5 mu`handis ga`Siir	10 ktaab kbiir

Exercise 7

1 Sa`baaH in`noor	4 `ana min Halab
2 ta`maam. initih kiifak?	5 `ahlan fiiki
3 w ana ismi ismaa3iin	6 `ana min irbid

Exercise 8

Several answers are possible, as long as new vocabulary, structures and expressions are used.

Unit 2

Exercise 1

1 `ahlan `3ammuh abu khalid
2 `ahlan `xaaltuh um khalid
3 `tsharrafna
4 `ahlan wa `sahlan
5 `ahlan `xaaltuh um Omar

Exercise 2

No, nothing will change.

Exercise 3a

1 al`maani; al`maanyah; German
2 `ruusi; `ruusiyih; Russian
3 falas`Tiini; falas`Tiiniyih; Palestinian
4 `ja`zaaʔiri; ja`zaaʔiriyih; Algerian
5 mak`siiki; mak`siikiyih; Mexican
6 israa`iili; israa`iiliyih; Israeli
7 qa`Tari; qa`Tariyih; Qatari
8 is`baanni; is`baanniyih; Spanish
9 `kanadi; `kanadiyih; Canadian
10 3am`maani; 3am`maaniyih; Ammani (from Amman)

Exercise 3b

1 almaan`iyat; Germans
2 ruus`iyat; Russians
3 falasTiini`yiin; falasTiin`iyaat; Palestinians
4 jazaa`ʔiriin; jazaa`ʔiriyat; Algerians
5 maksiik`iin; maksiik`iyat; Mexicans
6 israa`iiliin; israa`liyat; Israelis
7 `qaTariin; `qaTariyat; Qataris
8 is`baanniin; is`baanniyat; Spanish
9 `kanadiin; `kanadiyat; Canadians
10 3amm`maaniin; 3am`maaniyat; Ammanis (from Amman)

Exercise 4

1 ana m3allim
2 hiih\hiyya m3allmih
3 intih\intah muhandis
4 intih\intah amriiki
5 huuh\huwwa lubnaani

Exercise 5

1 ihna m3almiin\ma3aaliim
2 3indi thalath sayyaraat
3 ana urduni bass huuh amriiki
4 heeh falasTiiniyih w huuh bariTaani
5 hinih kanadiyaat

Exercise 7

1 باب	6 بات
2 ثابِت	7 جيب
3 بتحِب	8 ثُوب
4 حاج	9 جوبا
5 خاب	10 حَبيب

Exercise 8

ا	و	ي	ب	ت	ث	ج	ح	خ
93	31	29	20	16	4	2	7	1

Unit 3

Exercise 1a

1 muna; مُنى
2 waaʔil; وائل
3 3abdallah; عبدالله
4 ibrahiim; ابراهيم
5 wafaaʔ; وفاء
6 samiira; سميرة
7 mHammad; محمد
8 yuusif; يوسف
9 manaal; منال
10 SaaliH; صالح
11 Sabri; صبري
12 imaan; ايمان

Exercise 1b

1 ax; Sabri is Wael's brother
2 uxt; Samira is Wafa's sister
3 Hama; Ibrahim is Yousef's father in law
4 um; Eman is Samira's mother
5 Hama; Mohammed is Samira's father in law
6 zooj; Mohammed is Muna's husband
7 3ammih; Manal is Sabri's aunt
8 ibin; Muna is Saleh's mother
9 ibin; Sabri is Yousef's son
10 xaalih; Wafa is Wael's aunt
11 zooj; Yousef is Samira's husband
12 ibin; Saleh is Mohammed's son

Exercise 2

1 xams shabaab
2 baabeyn
3 Seyf waaHad
4 3ashar ma3aliim
5 sitt m3almaat

Exercise 3

1 How many brothers do you have?
2 How many pens do you have?
3 How many girls are in the house?
4 How many big boys are there?
5 How many great girls are there?

Exercise 4

1 kam sbab fii ilbeyt?
2 kam ktaab ma3aak?
3 kam galam ma3 samiir?
4 kam muhandis fi iljaam3ah?
5 kam dular ma3ak?

Exercise 5

1 ʔawwal ktaab
2 thaani sayyaarah
3 3aashir Talib
4 thaalith Seyf
5 thaamin m3allim

Exercise 6

1 iliththneyn
2 ilaHad wa iliththneyn
3 iththalaatha
4 ilarba3a wa ilxamiis
5 iljumm3ah

Exercise 8

1 دُب   6 شِرّير
2 ذِيب   7 صاحِب
3 رُوح   8 ضَرير
4 زيت   9 نِسِر
5 سحَاب   10 حارّ

Exercise 9

ض	ص	ش	س	ز	ر	ذ	د
4	3	5	11	1	26	1	21

Unit 4

Exercise 1

1 fi iljaam3ah
2 imbaariH
3 aHmad wa xaalid wa salma
4 bi diinaar waaHid bass
5 saa3ah min maama

Exercise 2

1 haadha
2 sayyaarah
3 ahlan
4 shuu
5 fi

Exercise 3

1 mish; muu
2 mish; muu
3 maa
4 laa
5 maa

Exercise 4

1 3ala
2 fi
3 bi
4 min; la
5 min

Exercise 5

1 shuu ra?ykum shabaab nruuH 3almaT3am?
2 ilyoom iljaw Hilu.
3 katabti shi bilmuHaaDarah?
4 yoom ilaHad 3uTlah.
5 ana ismii muna.
6 ruHna riHlih raa?i3ah.
7 kaan iSSaff Tawiil.
8 balaagi ma3ak 3ashar danaaniir?
9 raH ?a3arfik 3ala 3eilti.
10 lijtimaa3 issaa3ah arba3ah.

Exercise 7

1 طَلَب   6 قَلب
2 ظَرف   7 كاس
3 عَرَبي   8 لوز
4 غَزال   9 فَريد
5 فيل   10 طَلَع

Exercise 8

ل	ك	ق	ف	غ	ع	ظ	ط
60	10	12	8	4	17	1	0

Unit five

Exercise 1

Main dishes: mashaawi; sheysh jaaj; xuDaar.
Appetizers: salaTah; muqabilaat; mtabbal; mHammarah; kibbih; laban;
   mxlallal, HummuS; zeytuun; fuul; fiTir.
Drinks: bibsi; gahwah; shay; mayyih.
Polite service words: SiHteyn; bituʔmur; bi3yuuni; taHit amrik; 3ala Tuul.
Polite responses: 3ala galbak.

Exercise 2

1 marHaba
2 ahlan shabaab, tfaDDalu
3 ahlan biik. bidnaa nitghadda, shuu fiih 3indkum ilyoom
4 haay ilminyu. shuuf shuu btuʔmur
5 law samaHt, bidna HummuS, fuul, falaafil, mtabbal w mHammarah
6 3ala Tuul, ay shi thaani?
7 aah, shay law samaHt
8 tikram
9 kam bikuun liHsaab?
10 liHsaab bikuun thaman dananiir w nuSS
11 HaaDir

Exercise 3

1 arba3 w thalaathiin
2 xams w xamsiin
3 sab3iin
4 miiyih w arba3ah
5 miiyih w thamaaniyih w sittiin
6 alfeyn w thamaan miiyih w tis3ah w arb3iin
7 arba3 aalaaf w iththna3ish
8 thaman aalaaf w sitt miiyih w thalaath w arb3iin
9 iththniin malyoon w thaman miiyih, thalaath w sab3iin alf w
   xamis miiyih w waaHad w tis3iin
10 sabi3 malyoon w arba3 miiyih w iththniin w thalaathiin alf w tis3
   miiyih w sab3ah

Exercise 4

1 xamis muHaaDraat
2 Saffeyn
3 3ashar ?ayaam
4 xamasTa3isher maktab
5 arba3 w 3ishriin saa3ah
6 thamaaniyih w thamaniin shagah
7 thalaath miiyih xams w xamsiin binaayih
8 malyoon dulaar
9 sitt aalaaf muhandis
10 xamis miit jaam3ah

Exercise 5

1 thalaath w nuSS
2 iththniin w xams w xamsiin

3 waaHid w xams w sab3iin
4 thamaaniyih w 3ishriin

Exercise 6

1 aba3a
2 sab3a w saba3Ta3shar dagiigah
3 tis3a w thilith
4 3asharah w nuSS
5 iththna3ish w xams w thalaathiin dagiigah
6 waHadih w xams w arbi3iin
7 sittih w arba3ah w xamsiin
8 thamanyih w xamsiin

Exercise 8

1 هُم
2 الليِل
3 أهلا
4 مَشاوي
5 كَباب

6 سَلَطة
7 مَطعم
8 الأردُن
9 كِتابَة
10 خُضرَروات

Exercise 9

م	ن	هـ	و	لا	ي
31	26	8	31	12	29

Unit 6

Exercise 1

1 ahlein fiiki
2 shukran
3 ilHamdu lillaah

4 yslamu ?ideyki
5 3ala galbik

Exercise 2

1 allaah ybaarik fiik
2 maa saafarit ?abadan
3 il?akil kthiir zaaki

4 baddi ?al3ab kamaan marrah
5 ilHamdu lillaah shbi3it

Exercise 3

1 3aamliin
2 ybaarik
3 ilHamdu lillaah

4 bitHibi
5 mumkin

Exercise 4

1 maa fiih ghalabih
2 SiHteyn
3 allaah ysallmak

4 itfaDDali
5 ziid, kul kamaan
6 allaah ydiimak

Exercise 5

noun – adjective phrase	iDaafah
العالم العربي؛ الدولة الإسلامية؛ الكتابة المسمارية؛ الدولة العباسية؛ للحضارة الاكادية	غرب العالم؛ سكان العراق؛ دولة العراق؛ بلاد الرافدين؛ اختراع الكتابة

Exercise 6

1 my brother's home   y
2 delicious food   n
3 a new house   n
4 pizza restaurant   y
5 the door of the house   y

Exercise 7

1 arba3ah- sab3ah-alfeyn w 3ishriin
2 waaHad w thalaathiin-iththna3ish-lfeyn w xamsih
3 tisa3Ta3ish- tis3ah-?lf w tisi3miiyih w xams w thamaanii
4 tisa3Ta3ish- tis3ah-alfeyn w xams w 3ishriin
5 3asharah-iththniin-alf w tis3miiyih w sittiin

Exercise 8

?akiid, tamaam, mumtaaz, Tayyib, ?akiid, fikrah mumtaazih

Exercise 9

	English		عربي		
1	ahlan toomas, tfaDDal, tfaDDal	a	ممكن آكل عدس و بندورة ؟	1	f
2	shukran, shukran. ahlan biik	b	شكراً، شكراً، أهلاً بيك	2	b
3	maa shaa allaah	c	ماشي، مع السلامة	3	g
4	marHaba saara, winta kiifik?	d	مرحبا سارة، و انتي كيفك؟	4	d
5	HummuS w falaafil	e	فكرة ممتازة	5	i
6	mumkin aakul 3adas w bandoorah?	f	أهلاً توماس، تفضّل، تفضّل	6	a
7	maashi, ma3 issalaamih	g	ما شاء الله	7	c
8	mumtaaz. shahr tis3ah 3iid ilaDHa	h	ممتاز،شهر تسعة عيد الأضحى	8	h
9	Tayyib. shahr 3asharah ilbatra	i	حمص و فلافل	9	j
10	fikrah mumtaazih	j	طيب،شهر عشرة البترا	10	e

Exercise 10

1 ana; sa?alt
2 iHna; sa?alna
3 intah; sa?alt
4 inti; sa?alti
5 intum; sa?altum

6 intin; sa?altin
7 huwwa; sa?al
8 hiyya; sa?alat
9 humma; sa?alu
10 hinnih; sa?alin

Exercise 11

1 uxti sa?altni 3an iltalifoon
2 humma sa?aluuni 3an ilmuHaaDarah
3 iHna sa?alna 3an ilbinaayih
4 hinnih sa?alin 3an ilwalad
5 baba sa?alni 3an ilimtiHaan

Unit 7

Exercise 1

kaasih, funjaan
tuffaaHah, faraawlih, leymuun, shummaam
?argiilih, nakhah, duxxaan, bidaxxin
maT3am, garsoon, Hsaab, danaaniir
shay, gahwah, mayyih, saada, sukkar, na3na3
salaTah, laban, mxallal. fuul
ghada, sheysh jaaj, mashaawi
saa3ah, dagiigah, tamaam

Exercise 2

btruuH dughri Hawaali xamsiin mitir, ba3deyn thaani daxlih 3ashshmaal
ba3deyn dughri Hawaali 200 mitir, ba3deyn bitruuH yamiin w btuuSal
3almaT3am, giddamug fiih suubar maarkit iljaam3ah

Exercise 3

1 aHmar, abyaD, azrag.
2 aHmar, abyaD.
3 aswad, abyaD, axDar, aHmar.
4 abyaD, azrag, aHmar.
5 azrag, aSfar.
6 Open answers.

Exercise 4

1 bukrah raH ?akuun mashghuul kthiir.
2 kam thaman haadha ilgamiiS.
3 haadha ilxaatim hadiyyih min xaali.
4 raH ?ashtari nafs saa3tik.
5 ya reyt ?asaafer 3alurdun.

Exercise 5

Verbs	Nouns	Particles
yxaliik, zabbiTTha, badaxxin twaSilni, iTla3i, nishrab 3rift, jaabatuh	na3na3, nakhah, gamiiS 3inwaan, Haraarah, shaari3 jariidih, sawwaag, dawa binaayih, hadiyyih	Hawaali, mitil, nafs, maa haay

Exercise 6

1 ?argiilih
2 na3na3
3 leymuun
4 Hawaali
5 mithil

Exercise 7

1 iththneyn w 3ishriin
2 sabi3 aalaaf w arba3 miit dular
3 xams w 3ishriin diinaar
4 bithalaTa3shar diinaar
5 sitt marrat

Exercise 8

1 kam thaman ilgamiiS?
2 gaddeish 3umrak?
3 bikam Taawilt ilsufrah?
4 bikam ilsandwish?
5 kam thaman ilxaatim.

Exercise 9

1 maa 3indi sayyaarah.
2 3indi 3uTlah bukrah.
3 fiih maktabih bibeyti.
4 fiih maT3am bihadha ishshaari3?
5 3indak shay, law samaHit?

Exercise 10

1 0
2 illi
3 illi
4 0
5 illi

Exercise 11

Past tense	English
3rifit	I knew
3rifna	we knew
3rifit	you knew (sing. masc.)
3rifti	you knew (sing. fem.)
3riftu	you knew (pl. masc.)
3riftin	you knew (pl. fem.)
3irif	he knew
3irfat	she knew
3irfu	they knew (pl. masc.)
3irfin	they knew (pl. fem.)

1 3rifit hal issuʔal.
2 3aarfiin 3inwaan ilbeyt?
3 ana ba3rif SaHib ilmaHal.
4 salma 3irfat trooH 3aljaam3ah.

Unit 8

Exercise 1

1 fiizya
2 ʔidaarit ʔa3maal
3 mumarriDah
4 qaanuun
5 Tibb
6 Saydalih, ʔaHyaa
7 fiizya, kiimya
8 fiizya, kiimya
9 ʔadab
10 aadaab

Exercise 2

1 taxaSSuS
2 Tawiilih
3 mawjuudih
4 shughul
5 Sa3bah
6 ʔattxarraj

Exercise 3

OMAR: Sleiman, what do you have today?

SLEIMAN: Hi Omar, today I have three lectures in a row.

OMAR: Wow! Three in a row? That is a lot.

SLEIMAN: May God help. What about you?

OMAR: Two lectures, but one with a new doctor that I don't know.

SLEIMAN: I hope he will be good.

OMAR: I hope. When do you want to have lunch?

SLEIMAN: I have free time at two o'clock.

OMAR: Done, I will pay for your lunch, it is my treat.

SLEIMAN: Thank you, thank you.

OMAR: It is my duty (don't mention it).

SLEIMAN: May God protect you.

Exercise 4

1 dhakiyyih
2 kwayyis
3 mashghuul
4 niswanji

Amani is studying physics.
Omar is offering a free lunch to Sleiman.
Sleiman is having three lectures in a row.
Khalil could give his bus seat for the first girl.

Exercise 5

1 maa ba3rif idha ʔishtarat banTaluun.
2 bass maa titʔaxxar 3almaw3id.
3 ma3 hadha ilimtiHaan iSSa3ib ma raH anjaH.
4 bass titghadda, btwaSSilni 3albeyt.

Exercise 6

1 haadha, haad   4 haada, haaDH
2 haay, haadi   5 haDHaak, hadaak
3 haay

Exercise 7

sanih; sniin
kaanat; ykuun
bilaazim; laazim
ʔalaagi; nlaagi
fi; min
sniin; sanih
yishtaghil; ʔashtaghil
naayimaat; naayim

Unit 9

Exercise 1

JOHN: Hello.
OMAR: Hi, how can I help you?
JOHN: Please, I need to buy a headscarf and a silver ring for my mom.
OMAR: Sure. What color is the scarf?
JOHN: I don't know, what do you have?
OMAR: There is red, white, black, blue, brown, gray, beige, pink,
       yellow and dark blue.
JOHN: No, no, I don't need it to be one color. I want it embroidered.
       Red with white, black and yellow.
OMAR: OK, sure. This is red with white, black and yellow, and blue
       with pink.

JOHN: The blue with pink is beautiful.

OMAR: That's true. It is so beautiful.

JOHN: OK, can I see the rings?

OMAR: Of course, that is an original silver ring, but it is a bit expensive.

JOHN: Can I see another one?

OMAR: Sure, here is another one.

JOHN: The other one is better. How much is the scarf and the ring?

OMAR: Both of them are sixty-five dinar. Only for you.

JOHN: Sixty-five? That is too much. How about fifty?

OMAR: No way. Its prime price is fifty. Perhaps for sixty.

JOHN: Still so expensive. I only have fifty-five.

OMAR: OK sir, here you go.

JOHN: Thank you sir.

OMAR: You are welcome, congratulations, good bye.

Exercise 2

SALMA: marHaba.

XAALID: ahleyn, tfaDDali.

SALMA: biddi ʔashtari gamiiS mgallam.

XAALID: 3ala Tuul, kam ilHajim?

SALMA: wasaT, law samaHit.

XAALID: tfaDDali, heyk kwayyis?

SALMA: mumtaaz. bikam?

XAALID: 3ala Hsaabik, bala maSaari.

SALMA: allaah ybaarik fiik. kam law samaHit?

XAALID: biarba3ah w 3ishriin diinaar.

SALMA: laa, heyk ktiir, ra3iina.

XAALID: mash, 3alashaanik bi3ishriin.

SALMA: tfaDDal,ya3Tiik il3aafiyyih

XAALID: allaah y3afiiki, ma3 issalaamih.

Exercise 3a

1	f	6	a
2	h	7	d
3	c	8	j
4	g	9	b
5	i	10	e

Exercise 3b

1 biddi ʔashtari banTaloon bukrah.
2 haada ishshaal limzarkash Hilu.
3 shuuf, haaDHa ilwalad niswanji.
4 3indi gamiiS guTun miiyih bilmiiyih.
5 ʔijaani xaatim fiDDah hadiyyih.
6 fataHit mashruu3 raas maaluh malyoon diinaar.
7 lgiit shaal saada bijannin.
8 abu kariim, illi bibii3 xuDaark ʔa3Taani bandoorah bala maSaari.
9 maa biddak tghadiini 3ala Hsaabak?
10 shuu raʔyak nrooH nishar filkafi shob?

Exercise 4

1 ishtari ktaab, ya 3umar.
2 shuufi film jdiid, ya leyla.
3 uklu falaafil.
4 ruuHi 3ala iddukkaan, ya ilizabith.
5 il3ab riyaaDah ya toom.

Exercise 5

1 fikrah mish mumtaazih.
2 laa ta3Ti xaalid xams danaaniir.
3 ʔamiiSik haada muu Hilu.
4 maa baHib illoon ilaxDar.
5 mish mumkin ykuun mitluh fi ilurdun.
6 bukrah maa raH ʔadrus 3ashr saa3aat.
7 haada xaatim fiDDah mish ʔaSli.
8 maa biddi banTaloon jiinz.
9 allaah laa ybaarik fiik.
10 bass wallah mish kthiir.

Exercise 6

1 laa, maa ba3rif ʔa3mal mansaf.
2 haada ilbanTaloon mish bi arb3iin diinaar.
3 laa, muu kwayyis iljaw ilyoom.
4 laa, maa 3indi sayyaarah fi amriika.
5 laa, mish mumkin ʔashtariilak biitza.
6 maa tishrab kamaan shay.

Exercise 7

1 laazim ?aruuH 3ala 3ammaan 3ashan ilmuHaaDarah.
2 maa shribit shay la?innuh maa kaan kwayyis.
3 maa baakul jaaj la?inni nabatiyyih.
4 3ashan ?aruuH 3almaT3am laazim ?aTla3 hassa.
5 laazim ?arja3 3ala ingiltra 3ashan ashuuf ummi.

Exercise 8

1a nabiilah raaHat 3ala issuug imbaariH.
b nabiilah bidha truuH 3ala issuug bukrah.
c nabiilah maa raaHat 3ala issuug imbaariH.
d nabiilah maa bidha truuH 3ala issuug bukrah.
2a xaalid w salma darasu Tibb fi iljaam3ah il?amriikiyyih.
b xaalid w salma raH yudrusu Tibb fi iljaam3ah il?amriikiyyih.
c xaalid w salma maa bidrusu Tibb fi iljaam3ah il?amriikiyyih.
d xaalid w salma maa darasu Tibb fi iljaam3ah il?amriikiyyih.
3a ishtareyt talifoon jdiid.
b maa ishtaraytish talifoon jdiid.
c baddiish ?ashtari talifoon jdiid.

Unit 10

Exercise 1

1 eyy, ta3al bukrah ba3Tiik.
2 aah, baarak allaah fiik.
3 eyy, maT3am ilquds.
4 ruuH 3alyamiin, thaani baab 3ashshmaal.

Exercise 2

BRIANA: marHaba ya aanisih, mumkin su?aal?
BYSTANDER: ahleyn Habiibti, tfDDali.
BRIANA: weyn markiz il?amal iSSiHi.
BYSTANDER: eyy, mish 3aarfih bizzabT weyn, weyn galluulik?
BRIANA: janb makkah mool. bass ana mish 3aarfih weyn
             makkah mool.

BYSTANDER: aah, makkah mool 3ala ?aaxir ishshaari3.
BRIANA: dughri?
BYSTANDER: ruuHi dughri la ?aaxir ishshaari3, bilaagiiki bley
            steyshin, waraah 3ala izzawyyih.
BRIANA: ya3ni ?aaxir ishshaari3, ba3deyn 3ala izzaawyih.
BYSTANDER: tamaam, raayHah tlaagi 3amaarah kbiirih, yimkin.
            ilmarkiz biTTaabig iththaalith aw irraabi3.
BRIANA: shukran, baarak allaah fiiki.
BYSTANDER: hala Habiibti, ma3 issalaamih.

Exercise 4

1	Tawiilih	5	Taaza
2	kabiir	6	Sghiir
3	ba3iidih	7	raxiiS
4	naDHiifih	8	mumtaazih

1 ana saakin biTTaabig iththaalith.
2 3indi maw3id bissafaarah ilamriikiyyih.
3 ishtariit leymuun min maHal ilxuDaar.
4 biddi ?aruuH 3ala 3iyaadit il?asnaan bukrah.
5 si3ir ilxaatim kthiir ghaali.

Exercise 5

1 muna raaHat 3ala markiz il?amal.
2 muna bti3rif ishshaari3 kwayyis.
3 idduktoor ?a3Taani dawa mumtaaz.
4 allaah ybaarik fiik.
5 ilyoom ?axadna arba3 muHaaDaraat.

Exercise 6

1 laazim truuH sofia 3ala il3iyaadih
2 bidhum iTTullab yzuuru masjid igjaam3ah.
3 ishtara maark xuDaar min 3in abu kariim.
4 binHib ana w uxti nshuuf aflaam amriikiyyih.
5 bti3raf leyla inha laazim tsaafir bukrah.

Exercise 7

1 imbaariH; bukrah
2 raH; 0
3 btil3abi; btil3ab
4 mish; maa\ jdiid; jdiidih
5 yruuH; nruuH
6 ishtari; ishtarat\ jdiidih; jdiid

Unit 11

Exercise 1

MANAAR: I am tired today.
AMAANI: Wish you recovery, what is wrong? What do you feel?
MANAAR: I don't know, my head hurts. And my whole body is tired.
AMAANI: Do you have fever?
MANAAR: I have low grade fever. But I have colic too.
AMAANI: Maybe you ate something that was not clean?
MANAAR: I ate shawarma. And now I feel dizzy.
AMAANI: Fever, colic and dizziness. You have to go to the university clinic.
MANAAR: You are right.
AMAANI: Wish you recovery.

Exercise 2

1 dammuh thagiil.
2 3ala raasi.
3 Isaanuh Tawiil.
4 inti bi3yuuni.
5 baTnuh kbiir.
6 sinnha Tayyib.

Exercise 3

1 ?axadhit dawaaii ma3i.
2 maa raH aakul min ishshaari3.
3 ma3i mayih kthiir.
4 maa raH ?amshi laHaali.
5 raH aakul laHmih maTbuuxah kwayyis.

Exercise 4

1 3indi ?alam shdiid fi ?asnaani.
2 il3nwaan illi ma3i ghalaT.
3 ya3ni shoo raqam ilmarkiz.
4 xalliina nruuH riHleh.
5 in shaa allaah bitSiiri muhandisih.

Exercise 5

ma3i ?alam baSiiT fi baTni, ?akalt shwayyit salaTah ma3 ruzz w jaaj,
Saar ilwaja3 shadiid fi baTni. Hakeyt ma3 SaHibti gultilha 3indi ishaal
ma3 duuxah, SaHibti gaalat ishrabi za3tar. shribit 3aSiir w nimit w
lissa baTni biwajji3ni.

Exercise 6

1 shwayyit xuDaar.   4 wala waaHad Tili3.
2 shwayyit.   5 kull; kulhum.
3 kulluh.

Exercise 7

1 akbar min.   4 akthar min.
2 akbar.   5 aSghar.
3 adhka.   6 aS3ab.

Exercise 8

1 agwa min.   4 b3ad.
2 aHla.   5 aTwal.
3 aghla min.

Unit 12

Exercise 1

Seyf: Haami, shoob, Harr, naar, sama?, njuum.
xariif: hawa, riiH, ghabarah, ghyuum, maTar.
shita: baarid, sag3a, msaggi3, thalij, fayaDHaan, barg, Hawarah,
    ghyuum, ra3id, qaws quzaH.
rabii3: mu3tadil, gamar, sama?, njuum, riTib.

Exercise 2

1 baruuH riHlaat ma3 aSHaabi, w bal3ab riyaaDah w baSiid samak (fishing).
2 ba3mal shay w bag3ud 3in iSSoobbah (heater).
3 balbis kum (sleeve) Tawiil w batfarraj 3almaTar.

Exercise 3

1	Haami	6	Hawarah
2	naar	7	baarid
3	barg; ra3id	8	fayaDHaan
4	shams	9	mu3tadil
5	thalij	10	ghyuum

Exercise 4

1 fiih barg w ra3id kthiir fi ishshita.
2 baruuH kthiir riHlaat fi irrafii3.
3 iljaw bikuun sag3ah fi ishshita.
4 fi iSSeyf ishshamis bitkuun Haamyih.
5 ilgamar bijannin birrabii3.

Exercise 5

1	ms; aanisaat.	6	dinar; danaaniir.
2	guy; shabaab.	7	minute; dagaayig.
3	city; mudun.	8	apartment; shugag.
4	class; Sufuuf.	9	cup; kaasaat.
5	office; makaatib.	10	address; 3anaawiin.

1 maktab idduktoor wasii3.
2 sho 3iwaan ilbeyt?
3 thaman ilgamiiS 3ishriin diinaar.
4 shribit kasit shay zakyyih.
5 xamis daggayig bakuun 3indak.

Exercise 6

1 ba3mil ghada ba3id ma ?arja3 min ishshughul.
2 baruuH 3alHammam gabil ma anam.
3 bashrab shay ba3d ilghada.
4 baruuH 3ajaam3ah ba3d ilfaTuur.
5 batfarraj 3atilfizioon gabil il3asha.

Exercise 7

1 il?ustaadh sa?alni 3an akbar thalaath <u>binaayaat</u> fi 3amman.
   The teacher asked me about the largest buildings in Amman.
2 ghurfit iSSaff kbiirih. Tuulha sabi3 <u>amtaar</u>.
   The class room is large. It is seven meters long.
3 mumkin ?attxarraj ba3 thalaath <u>saniin</u>.
   I may graduate after three years.
4 fiih fi aljaam3ah 3adad kabiir min <u>il?ajaanib</u>
   There are lots of foreigners in the university.
5 kull yoom 3indi <u>waajibaat</u>. ana t3ibit.
   Every day I have homework. I am tired.
6 fiih guddam iljaam3ah tisi3 <u>baaSaat</u>.
   There are nine buses in front of the university.
7 ana ba3rif thalaath aw arba3 <u>?amaakin</u> fiiha maTaa3im mumtaazih.
   I know three or four places that have excellent restaurants.
8 ishtareyt sitt <u>karaasi</u> li ilmaTbax 3indi fil ilbeyt.
   I bought six chairs for the kitchen in my house.
9 ummi bidha kamaan thalaath aw arba3 <u>xwaatim</u>.
   My mom needs three or four more rings.
10 uxti bitHibb <u>il?alwaan</u> il?aHmar w il?aswad.
   My sister loves the red and black colors.

Unit 13

Exercise 1

fariig: faaz, xisir, mubaaraah, hujuum, kurah, gool, kaas
laa3ib: Haaris marma, marrar, shaat, sajjal, mubaaraah, hujuum, difaa3,
    indhaar, tasallul, iSaabah, najim
muddarib: indhaar, naji
jumhuur: da3am, shajja3, mubaaraah, mal3ab

Exercise 2

1 biddak titfarraj 3almubarah?
2 xisrat riyal madriid Didd barshaloona.
3 raH tibda? mubaarayat ilk?as il?uroobiyyih bukrah.
4 laa3ib iddifaa3 kaan najim ilmubaarah.
5 ilmudarrib ?axadh inthaar.

Exercise 3

1 ma tfarrajit, jfarrajna, tfarrajat, tfarraju; imbaariH ma tfarrajit 3attilfizyoon.
2 zi3il, za3al, biz3al, zi3lat, za3laanih. amal za3laanih min sawsan.
3 marraat. zurit ilmaghrib marrah waaHadih.
4 gulit, gaalat, gulna. ana ma gulit shi ghalaT.
5 ?asaasi, ?assas, usus. mHammad laa3ib ?asaasi bilfariig.

Exercise 4

Ismaa3iin za3laan la?innuh Saarluh sab3 sniin mitxarrij w ma laga shughul, ma3 innuh illi txarraju ba3duh ishtaghalu 3ashan 3indhum wasTah.

Exercise 5

1 ?axuuy kaan yl3ab faTbool lamma kaan Sghiir.
2 il?akil bilmaT3am kaan aHsan ?akil ?akaltuh biHayaati.
3 kunna nitfarraj 3ala ilmubaaraah lamma daxal lim3allim.
4 kaan 3indi sayyaarah kwayysih kthiir lamma kunit bilyaabaan.
5 ?aSHaabi maa kaanu badhum ysaafruu 3ala ?urooba.

Exercise 6

1 baddi ?al3ab	4 laazim
2 laazim	5 badha
3 badduh	

Exercise 7

1 rasabna bilimtiHaan.	4 tooxidh il3inwaan.
2 mish daarsiin kwayyis.	5 biddi ?aghadiiku 3ala Hsaabi.
3 xaalid b?istannak 3alghada.	

Audio track listing

All audio tracks referenced within the text are free to stream or download from www.routledge.com/cw/colloquials. If you experience any difficulties accessing the audio on the companion website, or still require to purchase a CD, please contact our customer services team through www.routledge.com/info/contact.

Audio 1

Introduction
1 Introduction
2 The alphabet
3 Vowels
4 Arabic stress
5 Countries

Unit 1
6 Greetings
7 Dialogue 1
8 Leave-taking
9 Dialogue 2
10 Pronouns
11 Possessive pronouns
12 The definite article
13 Gender and number agreement
14 Listen and repeat – greetings
15 Exercise – greetings
16 Listen and repeat – leave-taking
17 Exercise – leave-taking

Unit 2
18 Honorifics
19 Dialogue 1
20 Common nationalities
21 Dialogue 2
22 Regular plurals
23 Connectors

Unit 3
24 Family members
25 Kinship terms

26 Dialogue 1
27 Comprehension exercise
28 Dialogue 2
29 Comprehension exercise
30 Numbers – 1 to 10
31 Listen and repeat – numbers and nouns
32 Exercise – numbers and nouns
33 Ordinal numbers
34 Days of the week
35 Dialogue 3
36 Comprehension exercise

Unit 4
37 Yes/no questions
38 Negation
39 Dialogue 1
40 Comprehension exercise
41 Dialogue 2
42 Nominal and verbal sentences

Unit 5
43 Dialogue 1
44 Comprehension exercise
45 Dialogue 2
46 Comprehension exercise
47 Exercise – popular dishes
48 Exercise – in a restaurant
49 Dialogue 3

Audio 2

Unit 5
1 Numbers – 11 and above
2 Tell the time

Unit 6
3 Dialogue 1
4 Comprehension exercise
5 Dialogue 2
6 Comprehension exercise
7 Months of the year
8 Dialogue 3
9 Comprehension exercise

Unit 7
10 Dialogue 1
11 Comprehension exercise
12 Dialogue 2
13 Directions
14 Colors
15 Dialogue 3
16 Dialogue 4
17 Comprehension exercise
18 Past tense

Unit 8
19 University majors
20 Dialogue 1
21 Comprehension exercise
22 Dialogue 2
23 Comprehension exercise
24 Dialogue 3
25 Demonstratives

Unit 9
26 Dialogue 1
27 Dialogue 2
28 Comprehension exercise
29 Imperatives

Unit 10
30 Dialogue 1
31 Comprehension exercise
32 Important places and services
33 Listen and repeat – important nouns and verbs
34 Dialogue 2
35 Comprehension exercise

Unit 11
36 Health and medicine
37 Parts of the body
38 Dialogue 1
39 Dialogue 2
40 Comprehension exercise
41 Comparative and superlative forms

Unit 12
42 Weather
43 Dialogue 1
44 Exercise – discussing the weather
45 Seasons of the year
46 Dialogue 2
47 Comprehension exercise

Unit 13
48 Dialogue 1
49 Comprehension exercise
50 Listen and repeat – sports vocabulary
51 Dialogue 2
52 Comprehension exercise
53 Dialogue 3
54 Comprehension exercise
55 End

Bonus audio

Only available to stream or download from www.routledge.com/cw/
colloquials

1	Unit 1 Comprehension exercise	23	Unit 7 Colors
2	Unit 1 Vocabulary	24	Unit 7 Exercise 7
3	Unit 2 Exercise 7	25	Unit 7 Exercise 12
4	Unit 2 Vocabulary	26	Unit 7 Monologue
5	Unit 3 Exercise 8	27	Unit 7 Vocabulary
6	Unit 3 Monologue	28	Unit 8 Exercise 8
7	Unit 3 Vocabulary	29	Unit 8 Monologue
8	Unit 4 Yes/no questions	30	Unit 8 Vocabulary
9	Unit 4 Exercise 7	31	Unit 9 Exercise 9
10	Unit 4 Monologue	32	Unit 9 Vocabulary
11	Unit 4 Vocabulary	33	Unit 10 Plural forms
12	Unit 5 Ordering food	34	Unit 10 Exercise 8
13	Unit 5 Numbers	35	Unit 10 Vocabulary
14	Unit 5 Exercise 8	36	Unit 11 Translation exercise
15	Unit 5 Exercise 10	37	Unit 11 Exercise 9
16	Unit 5 Monologue	38	Unit 11 Monologue
17	Unit 5 Vocabulary	39	Unit 11Vocabulary
18	Unit 6 Dates	40	Unit 12 Exercise 8
19	Unit 6 Revision exercise	41	Unit 12 Monologue
20	Unit 6 Exercise 12	42	Unit 12 Vocabulary
21	Unit 6 Monologue	43	Unit 13 Monologue
22	Unit 6 Vocabulary	44	Unit 13 Vocabulary

Speakers: Rana Mohamad Al Essa, Shifa Askari, Maher Labbad,
   Husam Haj Omar
Narrator: Rana Mohamad Al Essa